Spiritual Alchemy

Dr Christine Page

MBBS, MRCGP, DCH, DRCOG, MFHom

Spiritual Alchemy

How to Transform Your Life

Index Compiled by Ann Griffiths

SAFFRON WALDEN
THE C.W. DANIEL COMPANY LIMITED

First published in the United Kingdom by
The C.W. Daniel Company Limited
1 Church Path, Saffron Walden,
Essex CB10 1JP, United Kingdom
© Christine Page 2003

ISBN 0 85207 371 2

Designed by Jane Norman
Production in association with Book Production Consultants plc,
25-27 High Street, Chesterton, Cambridge CB4 1ND
Typeset by Cambridge Photosetting Services
Printed and bound in Great Britain by
the Cromwell Press, Trowbridge, Wilts.

Contents

Introduction

The Time to Remember

The Ancient People all agree on one thing: we are in the period of the Great Shift. Some would say that it started as far back as the 60s. But certainly by the time of the Harmonic Convergence in 1987 many of us were sensing a change in our priorities as a deeper yearning emerged from within our souls; *it was time to remember and reconnect.*

As we move towards another important date, 21st December 2012, the end of the Mayan calendar, we must wonder what this highly evolved civilization knew of our time and what they would think of their offspring 5,000 years after the creation of their magnificent calendar. Would they have seen that, in the first years of the 21st century, momentous events would shake the very fabric of every society, acting as the catalyst for the transformation that is crucial to the evolution of human civilization and consciousness?

One thing they would certainly say is that these changes will happen whether you or I are ready or not. Because for once this is not about us as individuals or even a particular culture, religion or country. This is about our Earth, a vital being in its own right, raising its frequency to join with the other planets so that our solar

Introduction

system can take its place in the greater scheme of the galaxy and the Universe; this is its destiny.

As the shift occurs, we can choose to accompany the change in frequency by expanding our own consciousness both individually and as a group, thereby easing and facilitating the transition, or we can decide to stay where we are. Whatever our decision, the train is on the move and it's just a matter of choice whether we wish to make the journey in a comfortable seat or run behind the carriage most of the way.

We are seen to be at the midpoint of a 26,000-year cycle when the axis of the earth is perpendicular to the axis of the galaxy, creating an equilateral cross and signifying our shift from individualization to unification. Within this Great Cycle, our present age of Aquarius heralds in times of greater co-operation, soul opportunities, joy and harmony. But during the transition there will also be those who desire to maintain the separation to protect their own self-interests by evoking fear, poverty and suffering. This is prophesied to be particularly relevant until the year 2025, after which time the old order will start to dissipate, and those who are willing to hold a higher vibration will weave the web of creative harmony for the forthcoming sixth human root race. Some of these souls are already incarnating, bringing joy, remembrance of their divine essence, wisdom far beyond their years and other higher qualities of the human spirit.

So in essence this is a time for choices, allowing every individual to decide where they wish to direct their attention, and in particular their heart and mind; it's an opportunity to encourage the awakening consciousness and bring to fruition the creation of one's own destiny.

And that is why we need to re-member, to draw back into our being those parts of the self which have become separated or from which we have become disassociated through fear, ignorance or shame. Only by reuniting these various frequencies into a force of accord and acceptance will we organize and strengthen our own

2

Inner Light until it becomes a laser-like, coherent power. Then we will become *alchemists of spirit,* capable of transforming undifferentiated collective energy into matter and then back into the collective again and hence establish our rightful place in the Universe's greater plan.

It is our destiny to be alchemists dictated by the very precise geometric design of our physical form and the intricate interplay of energies between chakra centers, subtle bodies, the meridians and our endocrine and nervous systems. And yet we have often failed to fully appreciate our potential, oblivious of the strength that waits within and preferring to seek security from outside. Yet the *force is truly with us* if we can just remember where we left it!

In simple terms, we exist within an ocean of undifferentiated potential or consciousness known as the *Quantum Hologram.* This becomes organized into patterns or form through the power of our intention or thought. The more conscious our intention, the more pure the form that is created. Every time we take an idea and bring it into manifestation and then allow it to dissolve again, we generate energy which slowly but surely increases the force and brilliance of our inner light, drawing us inexorably towards the state of enlightenment which is our birthright.

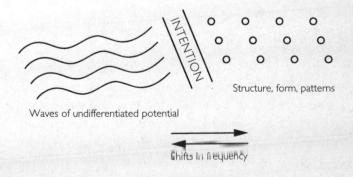

Waves of undifferentiated potential

INTENTION

Structure, form, patterns

Shifts in frequency

We are given a hint of the power of transformation upon our planet when we admire the exquisite beauty of a butterfly as it emerges from the cocoon or appreciate the gift of oxygen provided by the plant kingdom during the process of photosynthesis. And yet we must know that man is capable of so much more. However, at present, many of our creative endeavors are unconscious or poorly defined, motivated often by insecurity or fear which has a short-term gain and limited long-term collective planning.

As events unfold on the wider stage, we are being guided towards greater global consciousness which inevitably will bring greater peace. Already, I and many others are meeting the future in the guise of the *crystal and indigo* children who reveal an unshakeable connection to the Source, a true sense of their own mission and an intolerance of anything that lacks congruency. My heart sings when I hear stories of their compassion, wisdom and intellectual brilliance, presented without arrogance and in a straightforward manner.

For my part I'm here to act as a navigator to the extent of my ability. For as we expand our consciousness we come to realize that things are not as clear cut as we previously thought and will perhaps appreciate a friend who walks alongside holding a lantern. I will attempt to speak to as many levels of awareness as possible, recognizing the importance of each whether it involves practical solutions, emotional conundrums, stubborn thought patterns or the all-knowing eye of spirit.

Levels of awareness

As we take these thoughts a little further, let us create a framework on which to build. On one level we are living a *linear lifestyle* where thoughts lead to action which eventually leads to results; we go to work, make money, enjoy life and then die. Such linear thinking is successful and relatively uncomplicated, demanding little personal contemplation but requiring continual repetition of the process, as it is associated with few tools for memory and growth and rarely inspires the individual to extend their boundaries beyond the comfort zone.

$$\longrightarrow A + B = C \longrightarrow$$

Linear Awareness: "I AM..."

As we expand our awareness within the three-dimensional world of space (length, breadth, depth) and time (past, present, future), we start to appreciate the tapestry of life in which we live. We reconnect to higher vibrations that wind through and around the linear life, characterized by *cycles* or *patterns* which naturally repeat themselves and are reflected in the cycles of the body and the seasons of nature. Such a design linked to memory, the senses and our emotions permits us to learn and grow without the need to constantly repeat a situation, thereby bringing a deeper sense of rhythm and security. Habits such as riding a bike or driving a car are examples of cyclical thinking, allowing us to learn through feelings rather than merely by rote. Even the method of teaching words or numbers in a *sing-song* fashion has enabled millions to remember long passages of script or the times-tables well into their later life, as the arts are strongly allied to rhythm and memory.

Cyclical Awareness

A third level of awareness which expands beyond the confines of time and space is now being validated by EEG and MEG (magneto-encephalograph) recordings which show a steady **stream of energy**, the *Quantum Hologram* passing across the brain at about 40 hertz and is seen to reflect our interconnectedness to all dimensions. This waveform of energy extends beyond the physical form and is associated with the subtle energies found within the aura and whole-brain thinking. Higher frequencies of energy have also been recorded and are still to be investigated fully but are thought to relate to extrasensory perception and intuitive insights. This stream of consciousness is believed to underlie the *hundredth monkey* phenomenon where, once a hundred monkeys learnt to peel and eat a potato on an isolated island, every monkey achieved this knowledge anywhere in the world.

Collective Awareness

At present there is an alarming increase in the number of children with Autism and ADHD (attention deficit, hyperactivity disorder). Although each of these illnesses exhibits different pathology, there is a common theme that suggests that these children relate strongly to this third function of awareness i.e. they are able to see in pictures, merge easily with their environment, and often express telepathic tendencies. Most of these children find linear thinking and learning difficult, causing them to feel ungrounded and challenged to fit into the social norms. And yet, I sense we are being offered an opportunity to expand our consciousness through these souls who are asking us to meet them in their telepathic, whole-brain thinking rather than insisting on breaking everything down into a language that makes no sense to collective thinkers.

There is also an increase in mental illness reflecting, I believe, more than merely a chemical dysfunction but a change in the functional capacity of neural pathways to accommodate greater inter-connectedness and moving us steadily towards our inherent multidimensional existence. Rather than seeing this shift as a problem to be fixed we need to appreciate the magnitude of the change it heralds. We can accelerate its integration by paying greater attention to the value of the arts which enhance creative inspiration and by increasing tolerance for those who live by a different creed.

It is also important to restore rhythm in our lives similar to the rhythm of the heart finding time to rest, play and work in tune with a deep inner impulse.

At the same time, the future asks that we should re-establish a healthy co-operation with the planet and, with respect and honor, touch her gently with our hands, feet and humble hearts. It is only when we root ourselves within this world will we be able to withstand the winds of change, for the willingness to go into the depths of our being is directly proportional to the heights we can attain.

* * *

The irony is that, as we associate with multidimensional awareness, we're struck by the fact that the only time is *Now* and there is nowhere else to go except for *Here*. We also come to appreciate the ease by which we can move between the dimensions, for there is no separation except within our minds. To the linear thinker this lack of detail is seen as *chaotic* and to be avoided at all costs. However, the multidimensional thinker perceives this collective world as *real* while perceiving the linear framework as one of *illusion* and *limitation*.

This trinity of awareness has always been recognized by the ancient people and by those in fields of psychology who accepted the spiritual component. However, there has been a tendency in modern writings to demean the physical, linear existence and see the continuous flow as more important and more spiritual. The paradox is that such a view is a product of linear thinking, as it maintains a hierarchical system and seems to ignore the fact that we created this 3-D world for a purpose. What is important to remember is that, as spiritual human beings, no one dimension is more important for our journey than another. We are here in physical form to experience a style of spiritual growth that cannot be accomplished away from this planet. During this major shift, we are being encouraged to live in, move through and utilize all three paradigms of existence simultaneously which I agree is not an easy task. And yet, surprisingly, we have already been doing this for some time.

It is against this background that I will weave the words that will hopefully encourage you to repossess precious parts of your being that may be hidden in any of the dimensions and will hopefully set you free to experience a life far beyond your wildest expectations.

* * *

Who are you?

I recently experienced a moment of remembering as I walked along a beautiful, sandy beach with a dear friend on the east coast of America. The warm sun was glinting off the water as I expressed my frustration at a particular pattern of my work which after 20 years was no longer bringing growth and satisfaction to my soul. I was surprised by the strength of my emotions and knew that something had to change before I descended into a well-known pattern of blaming others for my feelings of restriction! At that moment I looked down and saw that my name label had fallen out, leaving an empty holder. However, not particularly perturbed, we continued walking.

About 30 minutes later we were returning along the same stretch of beach when my friend asked me what I really wanted to do. I became very animated by the question and said, *"I know there are parts of me that I'm not embracing because they don't fit into the model of acceptability and I'm not sure how to explain them clearly. But it feels as if I must express what's going on inside for the sake of my soul's sanity!"* This statement was very real to me because, all my life, the one thing that has brought me inner security has been the ability to take new and somewhat esoteric ideas and translate them into a language that brought some understanding to my listeners. However, now I was having difficulty understanding them myself as the ideas were so multidimensional that they lost their viability as soon as I tried to label them or squeeze them into the box.

In the seconds that it took to say these words, I saw myself standing in front of a doorway with the door fully open, beyond which was a world that was so expansive that I was awestruck but knew without question that it was time to walk into my own destiny, fearless that my logical mind couldn't feel the sides of the container and that I may not make "sense" to others, even my friends and family.

"This is who I am!" I exclaimed and, at that moment, I looked down and there was my name badge, lying face down in the sand revealing a virgin surface waiting for me to design my own identity.

Now is the time to remove the veils of separation, dissolving the myths that to be human is to belong to a lesser race or that each of us isn't in a position to know Divine consciousness. So I ask you, *"What part of your soul is waiting in the shadows to be acknowledged? What dreams, aspirations or beliefs about yourself have you carried from childhood but now lie dormant, marginalized by a busy schedule or, in my case, because they don't make sense?"*

It takes courage and a well-developed and integrated ego to step up to the line for oneself but it's worth the effort. It's so easy to remain asleep, hypnotized by those who know how to seduce you into a false sense of security whilst denying you your birthright, which is the opportunity to become a truly spiritualized human being. Interestingly, the very word human can be broken down into symbols that describe our Universal purpose: *hu* meaning *creative energy*, and *man* meaning *mind*. We are to use the creative energy of the mind, our intention, to become masters of the art of materialization and de-materialization and truly perform spiritual alchemy.

This at first may sound complicated. But let me assure you that you're already well-qualified in the subject, except most of your manifestations and their opposites have previously come from the unconscious mind, which then provides little opportunity to recognize and celebrate the skill. In fact the whole principle of *synchronicity* relies on this ability, so that when we think of someone and they call we're impressed with the instant response. Of course, we're less enthusiastic when we think of someone we prefer not to meet and promptly bump into them as we turn the next corner. Then we call it *bad luck!*

As the Ancient People would say, *"It has taken us many thousands of lifetimes to be able to create a physical form through which the soul can live out its journey and now we're working at de-materialization."*

We are no longer evolving, we are dissolving!

Perhaps a little history would help to clarify the situation. It is said that there have been four root races of human existence on this Earth before our present, Aryan, fifth race. The first two human models were ethereal, that is, without a physical body as we know it, and exhibiting androgeny within a very high-frequency energy field. It was not until the **Lemurian Age**, the third root race some

100,000 years ago, that separation occurred into two genders and the principle of duality began. During this time, the Earth was covered in a fine mist for our connection to the world of spirit via the etheric body of the planet was still strong and we were more comfortable in the oceans than on dry land. The physical body would have looked almost transparent as its energy was still of a high frequency allowing easy exchange of light consciousness and thought between people, the Nature Kingdoms and those of the Spirit world.

It is said that many of the magnificent ancient temples of Southern and Central America were built by Lemurians who were tall in comparison with modern-day man and knew how to use vibration to cut and carry the stones which today appear so heavy. We believe that the main civilization of Lemuria, which reached its peak about 54,000 years ago, existed in the area of the Pacific Ocean encompassing the West Coast of America as far inland as the State of Arizona, the Hawaiian Islands, the west coast of Central and South America, Easter Island, New Zealand and the Polynesian Islands.

As we moved into the fourth root race, the **Atlantean Era**, the mist began to clear with the vibration of the Earth's energy slowing down sufficiently to allow a world of matter to form and for humans to develop what we would describe as a physical body. You will probably appreciate that the *Big Bang Theory* follows a very similar theme with the physical world appearing as the ejected material cooled down. It's interesting to note that, every few months, scientists have to revise their estimate of the length of man's inhabitance on this planet due to the availability of exciting new data, causing many history texts to become out of date.

The location of Atlantis is still hotly disputed, with some believing that it stretched from Greece to the Azores, others preferring to place it amongst the Caribbean Islands, and some even believing that it is buried beneath the Antarctic Ice Mass.

Wherever it existed it was a highly technologically advanced society with many achievements far outstripping anything we see today, with a profound understanding of energy and light in its purest form. For human evolution it was a time to develop an inner power source distinct from what had previously been supplied by the collective universal well, which was then less readily available. It didn't take long to realize that the elements, fire, water, air and earth, could be manipulated into emotions and provide a powerful source of fuel still used today to manifest desires, i.e. anger, sadness, fear and joy. The Atlanteans also harnessed the elements into solar, wind, wave and crystal/gem power and became masters of creating their reality even though some of their practices and motives eventually became somewhat questionable and probably led to their downfall.

To me, this steady disconnection from the unified field was an essential part of the plan to bring about self-individualization and allow the emergence of human beings who were willing partners in the creative cycle. There was no mistake, failure or error in this carefully organized strategy except in the eyes of those who wished to exploit the situation, calling it *our fall from grace*. Only by slowing our energy to this particular vibration and creating the time/space paradigm could we explore and experience areas of creativity which were unavailable elsewhere.

Now in the fifth root race of the **Aryan Era** we're moving back to the source, using the very inner consciousness that created individualization to now remember and re-establish unity. Unlike the Atlantean Age, which was one of emotional and psychic development, this Age is focused around mental abilities, namely the will, intention and higher intellect, better known as intuition. It's time to gain wisdom from our experiences and to release our attachment to the world of matter that we have spent so many lifetimes learning to manifest.

During the process of individualization, we were like teenagers leaving home for the first time and were given two special gifts to symbolize our journey. The first was free will linked to *self-consciousness*, allowing us to become master of our own thoughts and actions, very similar to receiving a credit card with limited restrictions. However, as you can imagine, using this gift without proper care and attention created its own problems, as many became victim to their own thoughts either tying themselves up in limiting belief systems or becoming lost in free-floating anxiety or *monkey mind*. The other offering was the time/space paradigm anticipated to provide a secure basis for our thoughts to take root. However, once again, complications arose when time became the enemy and space an overpriced asset.

As Alice Bailey said,

"We tried to fit the Truth into the Hour rather than the Hour into the Truth."

* * *

It takes effort to remain awake and not fall back into the trance but now, more than ever before, the veils between the dimensions are extremely thin, and those of the spirit world who love and support us are meeting us in our dreams and meditations, offering encouragement and guidance at this crucial moment in our evolution.

As always there will also be physical messengers and prophets who will appear to help us with our decision-making, although now in this Age it's more important than ever to listen, not only to their advice, but also to tap into the wisdom of the soul, respect the deeper feelings of the heart, and follow only what resonates with the truth that lies within.

In this way we can appreciate and utilize the gift of logic while recognizing that our thoughts and beliefs can become distorted by fears such as those of change, failure or loss of control. We can also value our emotions for the powerful way in which they allow us to interact with the world, while remembering that when we become their slave and not their master, their *addictive qualities* can lead us into reactive behavior which will eventually undermine our actions.

The pure heart and mind never lie!

As the emotions become balanced and our minds clear and open, we start to remember who we are, beyond our name, nationality and the drama we're playing out in the moment. Indeed as the light starts to dawn and our perception of ourselves expands, we may see that what we considered a safe haven in our life has become a prison maintaining a false sense of security while denying our ability to experience our soul's full potential.

Once we begin to remember, our confidence rises, spurred on by the encouragement of our own inner self which delights in our awakening. This expansion in consciousness is reflected in the external world through technology such as the internet, which has given great joy to many through the ability to communicate on diverse and often controversial subjects and to hear the dreams and aspirations of others, all around the globe.

It is also time to remember that everything exists in this Universe as energy vibrating at various speeds and that heightened consciousness comes from being able to appreciate our own energetic nature and use the mind and breath to move through the various dimensions. As we move back towards our energetic essence, you will see a shift in interest from the use of dead fossil fuels to those which are more natural and alive, including the use of super-spin gold, the earth's energy lines, solar energy and sub-atomic particles.

We will also see a resurgence of interest in ideas that are an essential part of our heritage and without which we can never fully know ourselves and yet which have been banished to the realms of paganism especially over the past 2,000 years. Such age-old concepts and traditions as reincarnation, astrology, numerology, the world of spirit, subtle energies, the Nature Kingdoms, Earth energies, sacred geometry and the existence of extraterrestrial life can no longer be relegated to the shelves of metaphysics or science fiction but need to take their place amongst mainstream history, geography, physics and medicine.

As we assimilate these topics and others into our collective awareness through daily experience, we'll find ourselves closer to our true being and to a deeper connection with the planet Earth, Universal Consciousness and the multidimensional world of spirit. The only problem I perceive is that, once we reconnect to our own source of Divine Truth, those who consider their role as an authority figure to society will be required to communicate in a more honest and reciprocal manner based on a true democratic process where no one individual is more valuable than another.

If I look at my own profession I know that, like many of my colleagues, I entered medical school believing, in my naivety, or perhaps arrogance, that at the completion of the five-year training I would have in my medicine bag all the tools necessary to deliver healing to the world. Of course, it didn't take long to realize that not only did I not heal people (I was only the facilitator) but there was far more to a human being than purely their physical form.

I came to appreciate that if I was to become a true scientist, I had to be willing to go beyond the confines of my training and seek the mystery of health where mind, body and spirit worked in unison. I learnt to step back, listen and observe (not easy for someone who was trained to give their opinion and diagnosis) and soon realized that the complexity of health and disease reached far outside the boundaries of one individual. I would watch in awe as situations unfolded because of one person's illness and how the real healing occurred often subtly on an energy level, touching many people including the medical staff.

Sean's life scanned a mere nine days but brought together an estranged family after almost 20 years. He was born with multiple congenital abnormalities and was not expected to live. The young parents were naturally distraught and were comforted by the child's grandparents. However, there was a deep rift between members of the next generation who had ceased communication after falling out over a relatively minor incident.

Somehow the pain of the parents and the courageous efforts by this little soul to remain on the Earth broke through the steel reserve of the elders and one by one they appeared at the child's cot until the whole family were present. Within an hour, Sean's soul passed over, his mission completed. This story was told to me by one of the relatives who subsequently showed me some of the photos from the funeral. One particular image will stay in my mind for ever, for instead of a picture of the grave and the flowers, all that was seen was a brilliant white light symbolizing Sean's true spirit nature and a job well done.

* * *

So, mindful of the infinite wonder of the Universe, the focus of my work in the past 10 years has revolved around helping individuals to achieve health and hence wholeness through following their own intuition, drawing them closer to living their true life purpose. With intuition as the navigator of the soul, I often find myself as the facilitator of journeys that consistently refuse to stay within the confines of this one 3D existence. Ever trustful of the process, I observe with reverence as an amazing breadth and depth of consciousness emerges from the mind of one single individual.

I have come to realize that *if it can be thought* then it must exist somewhere in universal awareness and therefore can no longer be confined to the sphere of fantasy or delusion. How often I hear the dying speak of seeing, standing at the bottom of their bed, those who have already passed over such as their mother or loving partner. Even where there is no previous spiritual belief, I rarely encounter doubt in their mind but rather a sense of inner peace, despite the skepticism of a few of the healthcare professionals who prefer to relegate the occurrence to the side effects of the drugs or the disease state. Stories such as these may not be understood but exist somewhere in consciousness in normally sane individuals who just happen to be releasing the bonds of reality as we know it as they enter a new phase called death.

At the other end of the scale, I studied the stories of children who, unlimited by the conventions of what is acceptable and what is not, share their memories of other lives with great authority and consistency, often using words that belong to another age or at least to the vocabulary of adults. The stories given below were sent to me when I was inspired to write a book on the subject but after a while found that the true purpose was to open my own mind to a place of *innocence*, so that I could experience *in-no-sense* and discover *inner sense*.

I have selected these four tales as they show how such children can move with ease between time and space and even between lives.

Jamie's Story

One sunny morning before he was two years' old, Jamie suddenly said:

"Do you remember when I was a man and was killed?" His childminder, somewhat surprised, still had the foresight to remain silent, and with a look of compassion waited to see what would follow next. Jamie went on to describe how they had both been dressed in muddy green clothes and were chatting while waiting to run across the mud to fight. He spoke of an almost unnatural quiet with only the birds singing in the branches of the surrounding trees until the air was shaken by the explosion of loud gunfire.

Then he described them running and dying with *"bullets in our tummies"*.

"Do you remember my sweetheart who was my wife?" Jamie asked.

"No," the childminder replied urging him to speak more. He continued:

"Remember she cried when we talked in the garden before we left." Then after a short pause he said, *"She's mummy."* (referring to this present life). During the dialogue, he spoke in a very clear and steady manner, different from his normal style. He also used words such as chatting and sweetheart which were certainly not part of his normal vocabulary.

Months later he said to the childminder, *"You know that chatting has more than one meaning."* She looked surprised so he continued. *"It's more than just talking,"* and he ran off to play totally disinterested in taking the conversation any further.

When the dictionary of 18–19th-century slang was checked, a second meaning of *chatting* was revealed: *Chatting* was to remove the lice from the seam of the trousers of soldiers during the late part of the 1800s. *A chatte* was a lice and this information had been known by a little boy living in the 1990s in London, England.

Toby's Story

Children also have stories of meeting with souls who are still attached to the earthly plane but, unlike their parents, are less perturbed by the experience as if it was quite normal. Toby was three years when the family moved from an old Weaver's cottage built around 1750 to a modern 1980's house. His parents asked him what he thought of the move and he said it was a good idea as the *"fat walls (two foot deep)"* were giving him headaches.

Following the move, one night as he was getting into bed he asked what had happened to his sister (Toby was an only child). His mother asked what he meant and he said he was talking about the sister who visited his bedroom in the previous house. When asked where she slept, he replied that her bedroom was the attic conversion. The final part of the conversation was a strange thought for a three-year-old child. *"Did she go away because she was having a baby?"*

Quite soon, the memory faded and no more was heard of "the

sister". However, later, two male relatives confessed to feeling someone touch their arms as they slept in the attic room and that was why they had refused offers to stay until the family finally moved house!

Cameron's Story

This story gives us a glimpse of the life between life as told by Cameron's mother.

'One of his most amazing comments was when he was seven. My husband and eldest child had gone to football training leaving Cameron to cuddle up in bed with me.

"I really love you Mum," he whispered.

"I love you too," I replied. His face then changed: he became still and stared into space as if he had gone into a light trance.

He then said,

"When the men came to show me the women I chose you because I really loved you and wanted to be with you."

I asked if this choice was made before he was born and he answered, impatiently, *"Of course!"* I asked if he remembered what the men looked like and he said, *"No,"* before running off to play with his play-station. I was left to ponder and to be eternally grateful that he chose me.'

Robert's Story

It also appears that we can return to the same ancestral line to complete a phase of our soul's work if we die suddenly as seen in the next story. Robert's uncle died tragically in Northern Ireland, shot in the head in 1972. Before his death he had inherited his grandmother's estate, which was traditionally left to the second son in the family, and had moved his belongings into the house but hadn't lived there, leaving the place to be taken care of by the old housekeeper.

After his death, Robert's parents found themselves as caretakers of the house and it was here, five years later, that Robert, their second son, was born and named after his deceased uncle.

On his third birthday, someone gave him a soldier's uniform as a dressing up outfit and he duly put it on. One of the adults asked him if he was going to be soldier when he grew up. Without batting an eyelid he replied, *"No, I don't want to be shot in the head again!"*

Two years later, the housekeeper found young Robert trying on the clothes of his uncle which had been carefully hidden away. She reprimanded him especially as he slipped his feet into a pair of soft leather shoes, but just as quickly he replied, *"It's all right because these are my clothes you know."*

Robert is now 22 years' old and wears the old shoes regularly. He stands to inherit the estate which should have been his 27 years ago, had it not been for the bullet in the head.

* * *

These are only a few of the many stories which remind us of the vast nature of Universal consciousness still to be explored if we have the courage to step outside the box. Dr Ian Stevenson, a veteran researcher into the past-life experiences as told by children, has logged thousands of such stories. After studying the postmortem reports of the people these children claim to be, he believes that up to 40 per cent of birthmarks can be shown to be the site of an old injury.

He also shows that 40 per cent of the phobias experienced by people every day are connected to past-life memories, especially those related to traumatic deaths. The fact that *post traumatic stress disorder* can relate to other lives must make all those in the mental health field wonder at the tenacity of human emotion and the importance of clearing such memories if we are to find true healing.

* * *

As the time of the Great Shift approaches, it's important to appreciate the meaning of consciousness which, taken from the Latin word *scire, to know,* asks us to truly know ourselves and our world, not as an intellectual exercise but in a biblical sense, *to be on intimate terms with.* Thus it is by engaging fully with all aspects of Universal Truth that we come to experience total consciousness. However, here is the catch. Since the truth only exists in this moment, consciousness is constantly evolving within this world of time and space and hence there is, in reality, no end point to the expansion of awareness, it just is!

I smile when I hear, *"You're not telling me anything I don't already know!"* because it's probably true: intellectually there is nothing new to be said. Yet the beauty of this life is not to get *top marks.* As for the size of our knowledge-base but for our willingness to step into the unknown, experience life afresh in every moment and then glean the wisdom that contributes to individual and collective consciousness. The first step of the journey begins by becoming intimate with our own section of the universe which includes the reflection that looks back from the mirror every morning of your life.

As we engage with this process, we begin to *re-member,* recognizing deep within that there are "members" of the Self which are still disconnected and need to be called home as one would track down missing sheep until the flock is complete. During the journey, serious issues will arise and demand our attention as part of the liberation process. However, these situations are often sent to encourage us to seek a depth of courage not known before, hidden talents yet unexpressed or a standard of life which existed only in our dreams. Affirmations or positive thinking can help to neutralize strong feelings but it may be only when we face these emotions and hear their message that we truly come to know ourselves and simultaneously release priceless energy which dramatically accelerates our scope of consciousness and sense of inner peace.

Why would we want to remember? Because there is an inherent desire to know ourselves in all aspects of the self and hence to know God. As we increasingly acknowledge and embrace the wholeness that already exists as a blueprint within, we become master craftsmen and women, in other words, alchemists. Then we are able to direct the flow of creation with a conscious mind and loving heart, enabling life to become easier, more fulfilling and abundant!

Some of the phases of the journey include:

* Enhancement of our Inner Light through remembering who we are

* Perfecting the skills of the soul's navigator, the intuition, learning to trust its signals and guidance

* Appreciation of the different phases of the creative cycle and what needs to change to allow an ease of passage

* Mastering our emotions rather than allowing them to master us

* Liberation of energy which has become trapped in emotions such as fear, shame and apathy, and turning it into a force to be reckoned with!

* Cleaning the filters of perception until they become lenses of the soul

* Acknowledging all aspects of our being to the widest extent of its range

So here are useful guidelines to becoming a successful alchemist:

* Remember it's supposed to be fun and smile from time to time; too much seriousness is bad for your health

* Keep things simple!

Chapter One

The Purpose of Our Lives on a Soul Level

You may have heard a commonly narrated tale that suggests we're here on this planet due to a shortcoming which resulted in the original sin or separation. It goes on to say that only when we reach a specified level of "goodness" will we shed the shackles of human existence, attain pure soul consciousness and unite with the Divine, entering a place, sometimes called heaven, which exists away from this Earthly plane. This yarn has kept many trapped through fear, shame and guilt over thousands of years, unable to comprehend how they managed to become separated in the first place and fearful of honoring their rightful place in the greater scheme of things.

Now in the 21st century, information is emerging concerning these religious writings and how, due to the difficulties of translation, retrospective accounts and official human interference, the truth has often become distorted, buried beneath a mountain of mythology. Over the next few decades, I predict that more disclosures will come to the surface which will demand attention and will dramatically change the face of history as we know it today. Of course, there will be an outcry from those who wish to maintain the status quo but I suggest you examine this new research with the eye of wisdom and heart of truth and make up your own mind.

What is becoming increasingly clear, especially in the field of science, is that the world of form as we know it, is simply crystallized light or vibrating energy which has become organized into a particular configuration by the frequency of our consciousness or intention, our note.

In the beginning was the word...

Accepting this hypothesis, we need to examine what part we wish to play in this process, especially if we are no longer willing to be the Universal fall-guy. Even if we do develop a certain degree of self-consciousness and respect, it's easy to become satisfied with our little worlds causing us to fall asleep again to the enormous potential still available or allow the wool to be cleverly pulled over our eyes through the careful nurturing of fear, ignorance or smugness.

As we emerge from these challenges and accept the role of a spiritualized human being we are faced with a new truth which states that on some level our soul chose this particular existence and we can no longer look for others to blame, taking full responsibility for our decisions. This is a huge step for many who, under the *godspell*, happily or unhappily followed rules set by those who behaved like gods but who, in general, moved them further and further from the divine spark that resides within. If God is omnipotent then the obvious place to start to explore its presence and to see its reflection is within our own core and not within the mindset of others.

This may sound sacrilegious and I have no wish to trample on anybody's beliefs. However I believe that breaking this spell is an essential part of the remembering, allowing each of us to reconnect to a deeper, inner truth, the soul of the Universe, and essentially with the Oneness of the Divine. In this way we will come to experience the real meaning behind the words *purity of heart* which have often been translated as *goodness* but which in essence mean *to be true or pure to your own soul's vibration*, recorded for eternity within your heart.

> *It is time to be authentic and pure rather than artificially good.*

Imagine how it would feel to walk your path with confidence, fully conscious and without fear. Imagine, as in the Tibetan vocabulary, there was no word for guilt but only an appreciation that we are personally accountable for the consequences of our actions. Imagine if your thoughts, words and actions were not judged on the basis of someone else's dictates and experiences but on your own sense as to whether they resonated with a deeper truth within. This may sound too radical but this is the way of the future, where personal and inner morality guide an individual's actions, not man-made rules, fully appreciative that there is nothing we do, say or think that doesn't affect someone else somewhere and eventually return to us.

* * *

Knowing ourselves in the mirror

So let's look more closely as to how we came to be here on this beautiful blue planet Earth. On entering the ruins of ancient Mycenae in Greece, you pass under a stone arch engraved with the words:

> *Man, Know Thyself.*

Our destiny, as spiritual human beings, is to *know ourselves*, not just as an intellectual exercise uttered when meeting someone for the first time: *"Hallo, my name's Christine, I live in…, my work is …"*

But by asking the real questions:

"Who is this being named Christine? What is her vibration and what does she know of herself?" In other words: *"Has she sat with herself through all manner of joyous and difficult events in her life and increasingly deepened her compassion, tolerance and respect for herself and others? What wisdom has she gained that she can offer to universal consciousness? What does she now know of the Source of Creation?"*

We are multifaceted beings, similar to a flower with many petals each of which represents a different Soul quality or frequency, including aspects such as love, integrity, loyalty, independence, responsibility and service. These faces of the Divine, which spiritualized man is attempting to know and integrate, are found in all major religions and esoteric studies including those of the Ancient People.

As we incarnate into this life, some of the petals of the flower will be opened and fully integrated while others remain closed and represent the shadow side as proffered by Jung. Here I want

Soul

Folded, closed petal

Unfolded, revealed petal

to emphasize that these folded petals are not in essence negative but simply contain unexpressed potential and may include aspects such as joy, beauty and abundance, waiting in the wings to be discovered. Some aspects of the self may be completely unknown to us or they may be maintained in their restricted state through emotions such as fear or shame. Our soul's role is to unfold the remaining petals and hence know wholeness, a process initiated by our higher self.

One morning we wake with an idea, often out of the blue but with enough *intuitive and exciting juice* to encourage us to follow its direction. Without knowing why, we find ourselves manifesting this idea into a reality and *abracadabra* we miraculously experience a totally new facet of our being, recognizing skills we didn't even know we possessed. Then at other times we work more consciously with a partly folded petal to increase its expression in the world or simply enjoy petals of consciousness which are already open, tried and tested, all the while deepening our awareness of the self, its environment, the universe and hence the Divine.

In other words, even though we may have a mental concept of who we are, it's only by projecting that idea out into the environment and seeing the form and shape it takes in the physical world that we're able to appreciate our true nature.

By your Acts will you be Known.

And, it's only when that pure intention or inspiration meets its manifested mirror image face to face that we will truly know ourselves and experience an exquisite moment of bliss or ecstasy. Put in a different way, expansion of consciousness occurs due to the intimate relationship between intent and action and not merely through what we do or create.

When the action or form mirrors the originating intent
or idea then we experience an intuitive knowing that
we feel within our heart and mind as Ah-ha!
"I am that I am".

The goal is to recognize these *magical moments* of creative inter-course and hence be nurtured by the burst of light energy that occurs when spirit meets matter. However, on many occasions the originating thought is quickly lost and hence when the product actually arrives we often meet it with surprise or fail to recognize its importance. Thankfully our higher self is more observant and is there to welcome the newly unfolded petal until we are ready to acknowledge this *returning member* of our family.

This process of knowing ourselves is called *self-realization* or the development of *self-consciousness*. It is an *enlightening* experience for in the process of becoming more aware or conscious we generate energy which enhances the strength and brightness of our eternal inner light. At the same time, in a similar way that turning up a dimmer switch in a room will expose its contents, the brighter this light, the easier it is to see those parts of our self still awaiting discovery within the shadows.

So how did we forget who we were ?

There is a joke that says God created man because she got bored! Well, I certainly imagine we offer ample opportunity for divine and angelic amusement. But seriously, with the development of individual souls for the purpose of self-realization, there has been the tendency to fall asleep to our deeper essence entranced by the physical world we have created and all it has to offer. However, the memory of the Source and the desire to reconnect are inbuilt and hence each lifetime our higher self, the part that maintains the connection, gently nudges us towards unification.

What is not always remembered is that the only way "home" is through fully experiencing our life on this Earth and then, just when you think the end is in sight...oh, I hope I won't spoil it for you...shock of shocks, we learn there is in fact no *there* to go to, no *end* to experience and in fact there never has been an *Earth* except as a creation of our own mind!

But let's not jump ahead of ourselves, because each step is important to understand. Prior to each incarnation, we are given the opportunity to decide where to direct our attention this time and to make agreements with others to turn up at specific times for particular events and develop a sacred contract. Then, in order to enter this denser environment, our spirit body has to reduce its vibration to match the energy of the three-D world causing varying degrees of *spiritual amnesia* and leading us to ponder:

> *"Now, why did I come here?"*
> **As the little boy said when he was allowed to be alone with his newborn sister: "Quick, tell me what it's like in heaven because I'm beginning to forget."**

Today's children are thankfully far less prone to amnesia than their forebears, coming in on a higher vibration and hence retaining their universal connection. Indeed they find it very strange that many adults have forgotten their way, living incongruent lives where heart and head are not communicating with each other. These souls are here to remind us of our planetary purpose and to help us break free of the shackles of our lower mind and truly become multidimensional beings.

They instinctively know that it's through the fulfilment of their purpose they will come to know themselves and generate wisdom, *knowledge in action*. They also know that it's not possible, or indeed useful, to compare the value of one person's life with another as each is unique unto itself and hence to be celebrated. These children wonder at the logic of attempting to evaluate soul growth through the parameters of occupation, wealth, education or well-being for they know that none of this matters to our spiritualized self.

For example, a man lying in the gutter staring at the stars may be experiencing his last incarnation with only this one task to complete while those who *tut-tut* as they step over him in their dash to get to work may still have many petals to unfold.

> *It is not who we are or what we do that matters, but how we live our life.*

We are beings of light

When standing in front of a full-length mirror reflecting on how age, gravity and habits of a lifetime have left their impression on your sagging physical form, it's hard to remember that somewhere inside is a being of light!

However, the primary essence of your soul is pure white light containing all the colors of the rainbow, each vibrating at its own frequency and collectively radiating at the vibration of white light. This vibrating energy source, also known as consciousness, is a synthesis of the wisdom gained from previous lives, the energetic union with other sentient beings, the vibratory blueprint of lives still to be experienced and the eternal connection to universal consciousness. When the soul's consciousness is fully expressed, pure white light is seen, an event termed *enlightenment*.

> *Light is consciousness and consciousness is light.*

As our soul enters this incarnation it passes through the "personality cloak" which it has chosen for life with the latter acting as a prism, splitting the white light into its various colors known as the aura, each color representing a different aspect of the soul.

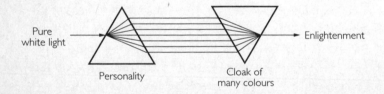

Pure white light → Personality → Cloak of many colours → Enlightenment

The goal or purpose of our life is to fully explore each feature using the personality provided as the vehicle of expression until a pure, coherent color radiates. When this occurs within all the facets of our being, the completed "cloak of many colors" acts as the second prism recreating the pure white light in the process of enlightenment.

Another way of expressing this is:

Out of the One comes the many expressing the diverse faces of the One and when they are fully expressed they naturally reunite, recreating the One.

You may now start to understand what is meant by the words *we are created in the image of the Divine*, for the journey we take from totality to diversity through experience back to totality is the story of the Creation. However, as with all good esoteric truths, even though day follows night and inspiration follows expiration, in reality there is in fact nowhere to go for despite our numerous excursions we have always been one with the Source!

Shades of color or consciousness

Taking the concept one step further, every color, for example green, can be broken down into a variety of shades from deep olive through emerald to jade, each with its own particular vibration of consciousness which, when expressed collectively, produce the pure coherent color called green. So to know ourselves fully, we aim to reveal and experience every individual shade of every color just as the unfurling of each separate petal of every flower is required to bring the rose garden alive.

For instance, if one of the strands of our soul is the color pink, associated with the quality of love, it's not enough to know love intellectually as a thought. We need to feel and experience it through the use of the senses located within our physical, emotional, psychic and intuitive bodies; *then we know love.* So from lifetime to lifetime we *choose* personality characteristics that will most effectively teach us about this essential quality of the heart.

But without knowing that love has many faces it's easy to feel betrayed when we find that despite our desire to experience *love,* our husband's idea of romance is to buy kitchenware for every anniversary, and our baby, now aged 16, is on drugs and wants to quit school ignoring our plea to consider *our feelings.*

"And you're not learning about love?" I ask.

Love comes in many packages:

* *Can we love those who we find intolerable, frightening or even repulsive?*

* *Can we love those who choose not to follow our advice or fulfill our expectations?*

* *Can we love those who choose to leave causing us to feel distraught?*

* *Can we love those whose words and actions are hurtful, critical or abusive?*

* *Can we love ourselves enough to walk away from a situation that no longer nurtures the soul despite the fact that others may be hurt and not understand us?*

And most of all:

* *Can we love ourselves despite qualities we would prefer to disown?*

Throughout our lives we are presented with situations that ask these very questions. Inevitably there will be times when the pain, hurt or fear is too much and we'll cry out: *"I want to learn about love but you can't expect me to love that,"* and we'll attempt to walk away. But wherever there is a folded petal of our rose, the flower is still incomplete and inevitably we will return to the same issue in this life or the next. We may attract the same players in different roles but the theme will repeat itself until we can fully accept that particular characteristic of love and the petal is unfurled.

The individual journey

As the soul prepares for an incarnation on Earth, it chooses which components of the Self it wishes to express and experience in this life. Some aspects will be those already well-known and unfolded while others will be those where there is unfinished business or karma within a "petal" still waiting to be revealed.

With the *fishing rod of highest intention*, the soul casts the line into the Ocean of undifferentiated potential or Light in its wave-form and clothes itself in a variety of personality characteristics that it anticipates will be relevant to that particular life.

It chooses a personality or ego whose lifestyle will lead to experiences that will offer opportunities to expand self-knowledge covering as many facets of the soul as possible. Since this is a world of consciousness where our intention dictates our actions, this personality primarily consists of *perceptions* or *eyes of consciousness* through which the intention will be directed. These perceptions consist of energetic frequencies, the densest of which is instinct while the lightest is intuition.

Take for instance the intention of honesty. When the perception is instinctual and mainly survival-based, the petal is almost closed and there is very little communication or connection with the soul. Any attempt to experience or share honesty will be shrouded by fear, shame and despair interfering with the petal's attempts to open.

As we direct more attention and love to this aspect of ourselves, the petal responds and begins to open, displaying perceptions linked to our ego desires with the soul slowly increasing its influence. Now we will view honesty through the eyes of our emotional body which will then direct our actions. With the continual light of the soul shining upon the petal, it opens further, revealing our mental perceptions around honesty and the beliefs that are defining our actions. As we refine these beliefs through continually reflecting them into the world and experiencing their effectiveness, the petal becomes fully open and the image we perceive is a clear reflection of the soul's original intention. Hence we know ourselves fully in this aspect called honesty.

What is important to understand is that our soul desires to experience itself on all levels, even instinctual, for here it has to stretch itself to be heard. In the same way that we evolved from a state of unification to separation in order to appreciate self-individualization, so the various perceptions are each essential to our state of consciousness. However, nowadays, many people have an abundance of experiences related to instincts and desires especially of the negative variety and it's now time to seek positive perceptions in particular in the realms of beliefs and knowing.

An analogy which may help further is to imagine the soul as a clear white light bulb and the perceptions as filters. When the latter are primarily instinctual or desire (emotionally) based, then the dense filters will diminish the amount of light that can be seen. As we focus on this area and use it to help us to move towards belief and knowing, the filters lighten, and eventually an integration occurs between intention and action and the filter transforms into a lens causing the light from within the bulb to intensify; *we know ourselves fully when our perception is clear and in alignment with the soul.*

* * *

To represent the aspects of the soul that we wish to know in this life, we select a physical body, parents, family, culture, religion, place and date of birth and even our name so as to be suitably attired for the path we've chosen. Each of these are expressed primarily as energetic frequencies and contribute to the perceptions or filters through which we will see the world and which will attract towards us events that will enable us to know ourselves fully. Many of the perceptions that we bring into this incarnation are from other lives and are merely represented by family and friends so that we can see them more clearly. In other words, it's not our culture or mother who has the problem, for they are simply a vibrational representation of a belief we hold despite their apparent physical or emotional affect upon us.

Remembering that on some level we are the attracting force for people and events we meet in life should help us to detach from the drama, not deepen it!

You only require a brief understanding of numerology or astrology to appreciate that where and when you were born, down to the last second, reflects your path and probably your destiny. I chose to be born on the 23rd of the month which is linked to flexibility, words, travel and speed. In numerological terms, it is said that my choice of profession could include acting, writing, sales or teaching but, whatever I do, I must be free to change!

If I then look at my family names, my father bequeathed me the name Page, meaning *one who conveys information* while my mother's maiden name contains the word Hawk which in Native American culture relates to the *messenger*. There is little doubt in my mind that I'm presently congruent with my soul's intention. As the Native People say:

If you have a name, you have a vibration and if you have a vibration or frequency then the purpose of your journey on this Earth is known by all those who choose to look.

That is why the sacred ritual of speaking the names of the ancestors is still so important to the wisdom-keepers of the world, for it reveals a wealth of information that is almost lost to any modern culture. The fact that in the Western world so many extended families are scattered and ancient roots lost, begs the question whether this may contribute to the fear, disconnection and insecurity that permeate our western societies.

> *Look at your own name and date of birth*
> *and see what is revealed.*

Many of those we draw towards us as future friends and family are those who have accompanied us on several other adventures over many lifetimes, happily switching roles frequently to add variety and spice to the experience. So when you meet someone and there is an instant connection as if you have known each other for years...you probably have. Out goes the cry, *"I've met my soul mate!"* Possibly, but it's more likely that they're part of your soul family coming back for another episode in the soap opera called life. What is often overlooked in the excitement and passion of the reunion is that our decision to meet again may be to complete unfinished business from several *unhappy* associations rather than to become star-crossed lovers. If she left you heartbroken and holding the baby in the past there is no reason why the pattern won't repeat itself again as it did on the last six occasions! Let's hope that this time the exchange of energy will be complete and everybody will move on fully satisfied.

Self-worth

Our ability to know ourselves through the opening of the petals is easily disrupted by an energy loss that all too frequently occurs due to a reluctance to remember who we truly are or because of theft, although commonly both occur at the same time. Yet, there are no mistakes or errors in the eyes of the soul, and from where we stand it's often difficult to fully appreciate that the hardest knocks of life can give birth to great courage and spiritual growth.

Energy and its importance to an alchemist will be explored in greater detail later but at this point I want to say that I've been awestruck by the strength and inner light that develops when someone chooses to call back their power having discarded it so effortlessly due to lower self-esteem:

Sandra *had such poor self-worth that it was easy for her husband and children to walk circles around her and have her dancing to their every whim. As the youngest of four girls herself and very much the "mistake", she spent much of her life trying to stay out of sight and so avoid the constant criticism that seemed to surround her. When she developed breast cancer, she believed that this was God's punishment for being alive and almost welcomed the opportunity to die. But fate wasn't going to let her off that easily and instead she made a full recovery which in retrospect was a turning point for her.*

As she left the clinic having been given the all-clear by the doctors something inside her clicked and she knew it was time to start the steady climb back from the brink of oblivion and to take back the power she had so willingly discarded in the name of guilt and shame. It was certainly not an easy journey, made more difficult by her family's reluctance to allow her to abandon the role that had caused them to feel so comfortable. Yet, she was determined and as she retrieved her power she developed an inner strength unlike anything she had encountered before. Despite all that had happened in her life, she was surprised that spontaneously she also experienced a deepening compassion that embraced not only herself but also those who had encouraged her state of disempowerment.

Why did her soul choose that path and that particular set of circumstances for her incarnation? Perhaps we will never know. But from a spiritual point of view, every time we have the courage to turn and face a new aspect of ourselves, especially one that brings with it compassion, acceptance and inner strength, we experience a flood of light consciousness into our being which is eternal and shines forth for all to see.

As we continue to call home those parts of the Self which have become separated our self-confidence increases which in turn strengthens the soul's determination to grow and expand. Without a healthy self-worth we are limited in the opportunities available to us and hence it is essential that we encourage this development in ourselves and others. As the Dalai Lama says, *"The greatest gift we can give anybody is self-confidence and respect which comes from a place of encouragement and love. Only when we know that for ourselves can we offer it to another."*

In time, as the perceptions clear, we find that the role of our little self or personality is complete and it gracefully merges with the matrix of the soul offering up its well-earned treasure-trove of self-confidence.

Science and spirituality meet

As unification spreads upon this planet, we are also seeing the coming together of the four great tenets of society: religion, science, philosophy and the arts. This is reflected in the work of the brilliant cellular biologist, Bruce Lipton, who offers the following hypothesis:

*Despite the fact that for the past 50 years science has maintained that our fate was preprogrammed in our genes, it is now emerging that our external universe, internal physiology and more importantly our **perception** directly control the activity of the genes.*

Hear again: our perception controls the genes and their subsequent production of hormones, proteins, enzymes etc. and not heredity unless the same thought patterns continue unchallenged from one generation to the next.

He states that it takes only three days for the DNA to produce a response to any new messenger (hormone, virus, antigen etc.) which comes knocking at the door of the cell membrane. This goes against the belief that our body is unable to deal with present-day environmental issues or new viruses. From this we can also conclude that the gene pool or our DNA is not static with its message set in stone but is more akin to that ocean of unlimited possibilities into which we cast our fishing line of intention with its bait of perception attached, producing a new scenario *fashioned in less than three days*.

It is obvious from this that if we want to change our biology and state of well-being we need to change our perception. There are many therapeutic methods available today that focus on this, most of which appreciate that, by addressing the physiology or instinctual behavior, the fear which usually underlies the disharmonic perception becomes transformed into positive light energy. In other words, when we are willing to search for the part of ourselves that is disconnected and is expressing itself through symptoms such as pain, numbness or fear, and reconnect to it in the name of love, then healing occurs. And the further we have to go from home to retrieve this part, the greater the joy we feel when we are reunited.

Biophotons as messengers of consciousness

It has been shown that wherever light travels it takes on the memory of its experiences, much like a video camera that is continually left running and then replayed many years later. Imagine the scope of information available to you in every moment as photons of light pass through your aura consisting of its various bodies of light. Like the DNA, our aura is not a static, isolated structure but is constantly exchanging energy and information with its environment thereby fulfilling an essential need of the soul which is:

To be nurtured by the connection and exchange of light memory or consciousness with other light beings which includes the Nature kingdoms.

In its densest form, this ability to exchange consciousness takes place at a cellular level when we ingest food, according to the German scientist, Professor Fritz A. Popp. Not only do we receive nutrients but more importantly our DNA (as the keeper of consciousness within the body) is constantly assimilating new information that it receives from light photons which have been captured by the plant from the sun. Thus when we eat food, which still has a life force present, the light body of our DNA receives information which, according to Professor Popp, is extremely important to the maintenance of our well-being.

Such information-gathering not only enhances the ocean of consciousness within the DNA pool but reminds us of the importance of remembering the interconnectiveness to all life which will facilitate our journey back to the Source. This explains why the Ancient People have so much respect for the Nature Kingdoms including minerals, plants and other animals, for they know that spiritual nourishment comes from the exchange of energy between life forms.

Remembering and Connecting maintain a healthy body.

Professor Popp's research has shown that sick cells emit more photons than healthy cells, for they are unable to download and use this information, and that cancer cells in particular seem to have lost their powers of self-identity and self-regulation, returning to their most basic linear function which is multiplication. I would like to present a hypothesis based on these findings and suggest that since this light energy is of a fairly refined quality it requires us to be sensitive to its presence to gain the greatest benefit. This can be achieved through the development of both a healthy self-worth and a reliable inner sensitivity or intuitive knowing. The former is related to cyclical awareness and the growth of inner strength through cycles of experience and the latter to collective awareness which reminds us of our deeper connections.

An associated experiment was carried out in the 1970s where two blood samples within glass containers were placed a little distance from each. To one was added an agent that caused it to produce antibodies. Within moments, the second blood sample produced the same antibodies even though it had no contact with the original agent. However when an opaque wall was placed between the containers, there was no cross communication between the samples, strongly suggesting that light was the primary messenger of information.

If light is the communicator of information and hence consciousness, these experiments re-enforce the importance of true communication and connection for soul well-being. In other words our soul seeks an exchange where everything is brought into the light and nothing is hidden. These experiments also highlight the fact that every cell expresses consciousness and hence has something to say which is certainly my experience when I incorporate *body talk* or *voice dialogue* into my work.

The body speaks

In my mind, there are few methods of therapy that get so close to the core of the individual so quickly as this modality. Here we literally dialogue with the body parts using the client's voice, recognizing that the body is a living, breathing, *talkative* entity with *devic energies*, managing the well-being of every major organ and system. Just to clarify, a deva belongs to the angelic realms and is a collection of energy that oversees numerous aspects of the physical world and hence are also seen in connection with forests, mountains, rivers etc.

Despite some obvious wariness at the suggestion of talking to their organs, most clients are stunned that their body has thoughts and opinions and, contrary to popular belief, is not the enemy that wishes to see your downfall but is probably one of the greatest friends you will ever have. As we start the process, I usually introduce myself to a part of the body that is in harmony so that the individual knows the baseline from which we are working and can return there at any time. I have also learnt that when we're angry at the body, it will probably refuse to answer, which is really not surprising! Here are some summaries of recent body talk sessions carried out with the individual in a relaxed state (not hypnotized) and talking with their own voice while holding their awareness on the body part concerned.

* **Jim** had been having problems with his prostate for months causing him to have to get out of bed several times in the night to pass water. He described his bladder and prostate as agitated. When we talked to the prostate it said, *"You bet I feel agitated. He never gives himself a moment to rest, fearful he's not good enough and always on the go."* At this point the bladder piped in, *"I'm exhausted being the container for all his fear."* I asked whether anybody else would like to give advice and the heart stepped up, *"Jim, it's time to enjoy life and have some fun. Go out and play with your grandchildren; I'm proud of you and love you"* With this, Jim started to gently cry and, having asked for the heart to repeat its message, I asked how the prostate felt and, the answer came, *"Much relieved."*

Later I heard that his frequent visits to the bathroom had subsided and he'd started to take more time for his hobbies and especially for his grandchildren.

* **Sue** had been trying to have a baby for years without success. When I asked the ovaries whether they had anything to say, they replied with some indignation, *"Nobody consulted us about the pregnancy; no, you just went ahead without a care for our opinion."* And what about the fallopian tubes, I enquired with some trepidation, *"Don't look at us, there is nothing wrong with us!"* Further conversation ensued with deeper (and positive) suggestions from the body as to the next direction to take.

It didn't happen immediately but, within a year, Sue was pregnant and this time every part of her body was included in the decision.

* **Joy** had suffered with persistent lower back problems for years and nothing seemed to improve the situation. We spoke to the back of the pain Joy was experiencing and asked whether there was a message as to why this part of the body was expressing the problem, *"My job in Joy's life is to support her wherever she chooses to go but I find she is constantly holding herself back with her fears, and frankly I feel exhausted. Every time I think we are making progress, she pulls back and I'm left holding all the unused potential."* As usual, I asked if there was a part of the body that felt able to help and the throat immediately saw its opening, *"Use me more as I often feel redundant. I can help to express your needs more clearly and attract the help that will support you when you feel scared or uncertain."*

Joy was amazed that her body knew her pattern of not speaking up and of refusing to ask for help as she thought she kept it so well-hidden. She realized she used her painful back to get the sympathy and support she required rather than expressing this through her voice. That day she vowed to communicate her feelings and let help in and *she never looked back!*

* * *

Body talk directly addresses the consciousness of the cells bypassing the logical left brain which wants to control and filter everything. As you see in the examples given above, the language of the body often uses phrases such as *pulling back* or *much relieved* which have a double meaning, representing the physical form and the individual. The messages are staring us in the face if we just ask the right questions. So,

* *if you have indigestion, where are you having difficulty digesting something?*

* *if you're having difficulty hearing, what are you being asked to hear?*

* *if your joints are stiff, where does this stiffness exist within you?*

And when the body speaks an intuitive truth, which the individual knows is accurate at the core, I often see tears or a look that says, *"Ah-ha,"* and that is when healing and transformation occur, moving consciousness to a new level of vibration. In this method, like many others that work directly with the source, it's not important that the individual experiences understanding through their logical mind, for you see the energy transformation through changes in their breathing pattern, a shift in their posture or by a smile or gentle tears.

This practice and the research findings given above, open exciting new doors for preventive care and highlights the importance of:

* listening to and honoring the body's consciousness expressed through the various energetic entities and recognizing they are often closer to soul awareness than our busy, little minds

* finding those with whom we can communicate and connect through a common theme or frequency whether found in the family, the community or friends

* developing a healthy self-esteem without which we are unable to reach out and make such connections whether with ourselves, other people, the Nature Kingdoms or with Divine Consciousness

* respecting all life, for only through this will we as humans survive. Nature does not give up its light energy freely but only when we ask in humility and with a view to co-operation

✳ eating live foods and not merely vitamins or minerals most of which have been stripped of their connection to the very plant that brought them life. It is through our ability to make connections or, in other words, *to love* that true health is achieved, and such a skill can never be substituted by the ingestion of a synthetic chemical.

✳ ✳ ✳

The edge of chaos

As we explore the quantum field theory we know that everything exists as patterns of dynamic, vibrating energy, the *explicate order* upon the ocean of undifferentiated energy, the *implicate order*, the terms coined by the quantum physicist, David Bohm. The interface between the patterns or structure and the ocean or chaos is known as the *edge of chaos* and is seen as a place of magic, transformation and bliss experienced when we manage to hold our balance between the two. It would be similar to standing on a bridge watching the still water upstream and the white waters downstream, or as a surfer, waiting on the edge of the waves with the ocean behind and the shore in front.

The edge of chaos is where the alchemist chooses to work, for here his/her intention can have a profound effect on the flow of light energy and the materialization and dematerialization of form. As students of alchemy, many of our creations occur within either structure or chaos with rather unpredictable results. However, our aim is to enhance our strength and concentration and hence achieve a stable stance so that we can maintain our balance across the divide.

When we do succeed in transforming light from wave to particle and then back to wave again, energy is released that changes the overall frequency of light consciousness and hence fulfils one of our prime destinies which is to contribute to the Consciousness of our Creator.

Living the three within the one

If we desire to master our own energies and hence achieve the balance required to become alchemists, it is important to remember, and here comes the mind-bender, that we are a composite of at least three energy patterns all at the same time:

1. The implicate order, or *streams of awareness* where there is no separation: *"I am..."*

2. The intention which exists as spirals of energy connected to the rhythm and memory of the soul: *cyclical awareness:"...that..."*

3. The explicate order, or the traveler on the journey experiencing different aspects of the creative cycle: *linear awareness:"...I am..."*

As a multifaceted being living within a multidimensional world we play the role of the writer, director, actor, audience and the theatre!

✳ ✳ ✳

To deepen this understanding, I suggest you focus on the implicate and recognize that in this state of consciousness there is no *me or you, now or then* or even a *here and there.* Here, and I use this word cautiously, we are the energy that exists outside the confines of time and space and permeates everything, just as the sun shines on everyone and the wind blows through every land without concern for borders and man-made laws.

There is no separation at the level of the waveform, for here there is only intimate connection known colloquially as Love.

To truly love someone is to acknowledge that connection.

However, we are multi-conscious beings due to the success of our journey from unity to self-individualization, developing intention and a physical form along the way. These provide us with free will and choice so that we can decide where to focus our attention and it is here that we'll find our existence.

Taking this one step further, it becomes clear that if everything is part of the collective waveform of consciousness, nothing can be judged as good or bad: it just is! It is merely our choice as to which area of the universe we wish to direct our attention and what energy we choose to take there. This is especially important when we intend to send prayers, healing or good wishes to people or places, for then force and focus need to be clearly defined.

Intention = Force + Focus

Force: If our offering is tainted by emotions and beliefs linked to judgment, pity, hate or fear or a willful determination to bring about change our way, then that is the frequency we'll send and it may do more harm than good in the long run. Shifting our gaze would probably be of greater service.

The force that brings greatest effect is love, which is not a nebulous affair but a willingness to merge, meet and connect without expectation or mental force; this is the state of *being*. An interesting experiment that reflects this well is when a group of experimenters worked with a computer that randomly chose whether to show a coin falling as heads or tails. Most people achieved a 60 per cent score of being able to predict which side the coin would fall. But those who scored in the 80 per cent range talked of merging with the computer and becoming one with its process.

Merging with the object of prayer is a way of truly showing

that we are willing to meet the individual at their level without judgment, and can only be achieved when we love ourselves sufficiently not to lose ourselves in the process.

Focus: The skill of manifestation involves the ability to be present within this force of love, holding an image and sounding a tone which reflects the state of wholeness which exists as a blueprint within the individual, place or group. In that moment we commune outside time and space where there is only now and everything is possible and our prayers become songs of gratitude as the effects are instantaneous.

Visualization + Vocalization = Healing

Jonathan Goldman *(Healing Sounds)*

Prayer is "successful" when we focus our attention to the point of interest with a clear presence and then…. detach from the result.

We need to be focused on the result without becoming attached to it!

Therefore it is inherent that we clear ourselves of attachment to the result, expectations, emotions unconnected to true love and a mindset that says, *"It has to happen my way!"*

Here are a few final suggestions to enhance the power of prayer:

1. Attempt to see the largest picture possible and have the courage to admit when your vision is limited and hand it over to those with a wider view saying, *"Thy will be done,"* or *"Let Divine order and Divine love work out."*

2. Be willing to look within to see whether there is a part of you that mirrors the issues of the person concerned. By healing ourselves we set others free and this can be the most powerful gift we can offer.

3. Pray to enhance what is already present in the individual rather than re-enforcing the concept of lack. For example, send light to stimulate the light that exists within the individual even though its presence is dimmed. By sending our own strong stream of energy we encourage their own light to emerge from the shadows reminding them of their inner resources and leaving us all strong.

* * *

And here is a final question to ponder upon:

If I create form through my intention, then who created me? Whose intention am I?

Chapter Two

Cycles of Energy

Stepping into the spider's web

In Native American culture, Grandmother Spider expertly weaves the patterns of the Universe right down to the intricate details of an individual's life and the complex culture of a tribe. She is the Guardian of the Creative Life Force, helping us to develop and use our talents while accessing our spiritual potential. She is the alchemist who assists us in finding self-expression and explains that, as we create circles of life, we touch and enhance circles created by others, benefiting all concerned. Yet we also learn that if these circles are formed in greed then we can become trapped by our own web as its strands are too tightly knit to allow sharing. And if they are created through fear, then the web woven is too loose and the circle will not endure.

Grandmother Spider is represented by the weavers and artists of a tribe who are highly valued for their ability to hold the creative force imprinting memories, exploits and traditions of the people into rugs, songs, and paintings which ensure the community's survival. Hence continuity is established through creating a vibration based on a common purpose and common past, informing the world of this particular group's contribution to the Greater Plan.

Today many modern countries and communities maintain this tradition with flags and costumes denoting a particular allegiance. You only have to watch teenagers to see this in action for, in their rebellion from parental traditions, they usually end up dressing the same in order to feel accepted by their new tribe.

However, as we unify on a wider stage, Grandmother Spider is asking us to recognize webs of personal, national or cultural significance that have been built on the basis of fear or greed and that are now limiting our soul's urge to connect on a more fundamental and meaningful level.

Let us look deeper to see how we, as individuals, spun own our web and how this connects to the larger webs of consciousness. In a 3D world it's appropriate to imagine our soul at the center of a flower with many petals, some folded and some fully opened. However, once we acknowledge our interconnected nature within waves of consciousness then the boundaries dissolve and the petals of the flower become streams or lines of energy into which our soul walks.

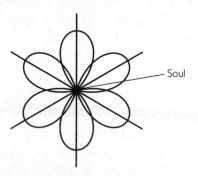

The Spider's Web of Energy

It immediately becomes clothed in many different strands of the spider's web, the creative life force, each strand representing different aspects of the self which include:

* Service
* Adventure
* Nurturing
* Mastery of emotions
* Honor
* Courage
* Curiosity
* Discipline
* Clarity
* Integrity
* Sovereignty

* Inner Strength
* Respect
* Receptivity
* Self-worth
* Compassion
* Truth
* Creative expression
* Responsibility
* Discernment
* Humility

Each of these core values finds expression in our daily lives through the various chakras which will influence our psycho-physical behavior. By choosing to be born into a particular ancestry, country etc., we agree to connect and often reconnect with a specific frequency of energy. Your parents may have given you a secure home and upbringing but more importantly they give you an identity or frequency through which you will create your life in order to fulfill your soul's potential.

What we then see is that what we relate to is not a physical person but an energy that has coalesced around our intention. Try telling that to your mother next time you see her! She is a collection of energy around your intention, which means she is a twinkle in your eye and not the other way round!

One way of discovering why you're here on this planet is by listing six qualities from each of your parents that you believe describes them best, including in your list qualities you admire and also those that may have caused you distress, especially in your early years. Even if you were adopted, look at both your birth parents and your adoptive parents as you chose the family not by blood but by frequency of vibration. Now, speaking in truth, ask yourself whether any of these qualities appear in your own life now (even subtly) and whether they are being expressed fully to their greatest benefit.

It may well be that your parents started with good intentions to express a certain quality but, due to internal and external circumstances, failed to bring it to fruition even causing a distortion of that particular characteristic.

For example:

* *From service to slavery*

* *From sovereignty to dictatorship*

* *From mastery of emotions to coercion*

* *From curiosity to over-analysis*

* *From compassion to neediness*

* *From truth to insensitivity*

Take my grandfather for instance. I remember him as a relatively small, aloof man who found social contact difficult, and I came to understand from conversations with the family that he was a strict disciplinarian who held the purse strings tight. But there was another side that I never knew: the man who lied about his age to enlist age 16 as an infantryman in the First World War. Whatever he encountered there I will never know but, from my knowledge of those times, he will have required great courage to survive both physically and mentally. Now recalling my father, his son, I see the same courage and adventurer within an extremely sensitive shell.

Did my grandfather develop his control and discipline as a way of protecting his own sensitivity against the horrors of war? And was this the origin of his consequent suppression of creative courage, causing him to become aloof? I'll never know but I see courage and adventure as two qualities that I have inherited from my father's side of the family along with the deep sense of justice.

I also know from my past-life memories that courage has featured many times, appearing in roles such as the warrior, the wise elder of the tribe who was called on to make difficult decisions, a widow left to bring up her children alone and as a child abandoned and hungry. I also remember times when courage abandoned me and I would then call myself a coward. But I have learnt that this label needs to be honored equally if I am to know the full spectrum of courage, for it takes guts to admit your fear in the face of terror.

As we step into the spider's web of creativity and connect with distinct streams of energy, we are potentially connecting to all those who relate to this quality anywhere in the Universe and are committed to enabling this energy line to reach its highest vibration through our life processes.

So every time we embrace another aspect of the self in the name of love, the frequency of that energy line is enhanced and hence every coward or hero is celebrated.

What I have come to accept is that my ancestors truly did their best in the circumstances, often keeping secure a gift or talent which they eventually handed down to me, even though they had limited opportunity to use it for themselves. There are many concepts we find difficult to comprehend with our limited lenses. This includes the fact that someone who causes us considerable distress could be in essence a spiritual friend and ally, agreeing to play this role because of their eternal love for us.

From a spiritual viewpoint our judgments and biases are understood and forgiven although it grieves our helpers to see us so lost in hurt and hatred.

Finally, if your siblings were also to list qualities of your parents from their perspective, you would probably see different values attributed to exactly the same two people based on their soul's perceptions. All are true and express the wonderful tapestry available to us upon this beautiful planet Earth.

* * *

The Creative Cycle

In order to take these qualities offered and experience the energy lines to their highest potential, we are continuously traveling through creative cycles that allow us to experience ourselves fully. The creative cycle is the fundamental way in which we come to know ourselves and hence the Divine. Its design is repeated throughout the Nature Kingdoms and through any rhythmic system within our body, including respiration, the heart's action and the menstrual cycle. It involves all three levels of awareness as described earlier, with the movement from birth to bloom and between bloom and death, reflecting *linear consciousness*. The completed cycle characterizes *cyclical awareness* bringing with it the gift of memory as one cycle spirals into the next. Finally, we remember that each cycle is only a very small part of a much larger picture which *streams through and around us* reminding us of the energy line on which we are focused while maintaining the connection to Universal consciousness.

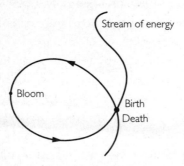

There are five stages to this process:

* **Birth:** We receive the seed of an idea which may relate to a part of us already known or a part still folded and obscured from view. Even though this stage may be

unconscious, it is often sensed as excitement, newness and even as anxiety.

* **Nurturing**: The soil is prepared to receive the seed and, as it is planted, its vibration attracts towards it what is needed to bring the growth to fruition.

* **Blooming**: We engage fully with our creation enjoying the moment until a point of completion is reached.

* **Harvest**: As the bloom begins to fade, we gather the ripened fruit (wisdom) ensuring that the experience of the journey is never lost. We celebrate our endeavors and then start the separation, releasing all attachment.

* **Death**: We offer the wisdom gained to the ocean of consciousness and the old idea or impulse dies. On entering the void or vacuum, we wait in stillness and peace for the next inspiration.

The creative cycle mirrors the gift of seasons which accompany the planet's movement around the sun. Even in countries close to the equator, there are subtle shifts of energy as the sun seeks a new position in the sky each day.

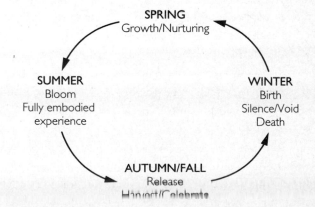

As with the breath and the heartbeat, there are phases of activity denoted by Spring and Autumn and then gaps or rests, Summer and Winter, when there is apparent stillness. And yet these still points are the most powerful times for the soul, for this is when energy is stored and when, in the case of Winter, we offer the light energy we have generated during our journey to Universal consciousness.

For instance, if my impulse is to experience joy, then as I express my desire I will attract towards me people and events who will help me to achieve this goal. When I find myself in the center of a situation where my heart is bursting with happiness, I fully engage with the feelings of joy. As the experience permeates into my deeper core, I stored the feelings as wisdom so that I can draw on them at any time. Once this happens, I can release the experience and fall gently into the void, awaiting the next impulse.

Rules of the game

There are certain universal rules to this *creative board game* which clearly state that to completely unfold a petal, every stage or base must be experienced fully and that if any stage is ignored or there is inadequate connection, then the cycle needs to be repeated again and again until the optimal result is obtained. With each successfully completed cycle, new energy is generated and the relevant power line becomes brighter, intensifying our inner light and allowing us to feel stronger, more confident and imbued with a greater sense of inner peace.

"Can I achieve all of this in one lifetime?" I hear you ask. Probably not, but you never can tell as we're always given the opportunity to complete unfinished business in order to expand consciousness. Therefore we meet with the same set of circumstances time and again through a variety of situations until we find a way of lifting the energy line to its new frequency often jettisoning limiting beliefs and fears along the way. But, remember, it's not the goal to simply complete the circle but to grow and expand during the journey. It is so hard for those who seek external signs

of achievement to appreciate the importance of inner work and the power generated when we face a fear or move beyond a belief that has foiled the progress of so many of our ancestors.

The result of our inner work is far more valuable to the soul than outside accomplishments, for in reality it is only the former that can pass with us into death.

Each phase of the creative cycle will present us with specific challenges which may have accompanied us from other lives, and it's useful to ask when you feel stuck or uncertain of which direction to take whether your actions at that time are being motivated by:

Fear or love?

If it's by fear, then take note and ask, *"What would I do in this moment if I was truly loving towards myself and others?"* Fear always paralyses the soul's growth and may cause us to stay in one phase far too long or attempt to avoid that stage completely.

Love may not give us all the answers but will provide us with a safe passage to venture into the unknown as if we are wrapped in the wings of an angel.

GIVING BIRTH TO AN IDEA

Do you remember a time when you were cleaning your teeth, driving to work or walking the dog when, out of the blue, an idea came to you and, for a second, an electrifying buzz of excitement passed through your body. You didn't know where the thought came from and you were fairly sure that it didn't follow a process of linear thinking, but there it was. You recall playing with the idea for a while imagining different scenarios and wondering which one would enable this seed to be brought to manifestation, and then your busy life intervened and the moment of excitement went cold but not dead.

All day we are receiving thoughts and inspirations which are circulating in the airways awaiting our attention. Some may be quite specific to us, resonating with our particular vibration, and others are general, touching anybody who is willing to switch on their receiver, tune in and download the information. The greater the excitement we feel and the more vivid the image, the more likely the impulse is directed at us, and that by following it to fruition we will come to know ourselves in a greater and more authentic truth.

Some impulses deal with our day-to-day lives, motivating us to take a different path or to speak words that need to be expressed. At other times, a fleeting thought causes us to bring to mind an event or friend who was almost lost from memory. Often the originating impulse is so unconscious that we may not even realize that the spring in our step has changed or for some reason we feel more optimistic. It's also not uncommon to have little true concept of the consequences of following such an impulse, for if we knew what we were getting ourselves into we may refuse to entertain the idea for another second!

Think back over situations in your own life that started with a relatively insignificant impulse but led to a major shift in life direction. For my own part, I remember reading a magazine advertisement in a library I had never visited before which caused me to spend a year working in New Zealand which completely changed my life. I also recall arriving late at a conference due to heavy traffic and finding myself sitting in the back of the auditorium next to someone who told me of a book which completely shifted my focus of teaching.

I've also learnt the hard way that pride and fear of inadequacy can greatly inhibit the download of a new impulse as in the past I had a habit of saying, *"I know about that,"* when in essence I didn't. Many great introductions to new studies would have been lost if I hadn't come to terms with my fear of saying, *"I don't know, tell me more?"*

The hardest impulses to follow, and yet the most urgent, are those which emerge from a place of deep yearning often surfacing as an illness such as heart disease, fibromyalgia or even depression. Such an ache of the soul, often buried in the name of social acceptability or harmony at any cost, commonly emerges from impulses that have been long denied from fear of failure or from facing the unknown. Without a healthy input of encouragement, approval and love early in life it's easy to become overwhelmed by fear, unable to take even the smallest risk. No long-term medication is as effective as the willingness to offer a hand of loving support and to celebrate small steps towards fulfillment. Indeed relying on pills to motivate and carry us through our challenging times may purely re-enforce the feelings of failure and disable the inherent strength that waits within.

It was many years ago that I came to understand how a sense of despair can be a powerful impulse for birth and reconnection. It started when I began to notice that, whenever there was a short break between working engagements, I would become overwhelmed by deep feelings of sadness which shocked me. My reactive impulse was to immediately urge myself into greater activity desperate to get rid of these uncomfortable sensations.

But one day something stopped me and I allowed myself to sink deeper into the emotion. From a pit deep within my soul, I detected an almost imperceptible cry of despair which wrenched at my heart strings. It reminded me of the story of the lost lamb whose bleat became more pitiful as its survival became increasingly compromised. In seconds, small streams of love were spontaneously radiating towards the abandoned part of myself and, despite a real fear of standing still and facing my anxieties, there was no alternative but to listen.

Months later, I realized that my relationships with life, friends and work had profoundly changed just by my willingness to stop and search for my *lost lamb* which represented a part of myself that I had previously believed unacceptable but now is an integral part of my life.

So I ask:

Is there a part of you longing to be heard?

Is it worth the risk to stop and listen to those impulses and possibly experience a change which could be the catalyst for something much greater?

It is possible to attempt to ignore the call and pretend nothing has happened but once we have felt the tremor of excitement in our cells, whether through joy or sadness, there is no going back.

So here are some questions to consider:

What is waiting to be given birth to?

What dream or idea have you had in your mind even from childhood that has not seen the light of day?

What enjoyable hobby has been laid aside due to lack of time?

If money were no object what would you wish to do?

What dream or idea are you ignoring because it's not socially or culturally acceptable?

What feelings emerge at the thought of sharing this idea with the world?

What do you fear could be the worse scenario of expressing these ideas?

What long-standing belief system may hold you back (once again)?

How do you already know you might sabotage the birth of this idea?

For example:

If I don't try I can't fail!

It takes effort to commit to nurturing the seed's growth and that's more responsibility than I need.

What if my freedom is compromised?

If I succeed, I may be rejected by the family; it's easier to ignore my dreams.

Some people are naturally creative and experience great pleasure implanting their ideas and watching them grow. But for others it's a struggle with old messages from childhood emerging as soon as they step forward seed in hand: *"What have I got to offer that is so important?"*

When the seeds of inspiration fail to become realized, disappointment and despondency set in. We find ourselves more and more reluctant to put ourselves in the position where anything new could be expected from us, finding ourselves making excuses for our lack of effort or hiding behind others, pushing them forward and encouraging them to plant their seeds but never doing it for ourselves.

Other illnesses, apart from those mentioned above, that occur when we suppress the creative fire energy, are those involving the organs of creativity such as the *ovaries* and *testes*.

Here are some words of encouragement:

* *Do it for yourself as if you were the audience and you couldn't fail to please!*

* *Make it fun, dropping all the heavy-duty expectations and allow the result to surprise you.*

* *Remember that the deeper your in-breath to receive this impulse, the deeper you are able to express it into the world on the out-breath. So breathe in and go for it.*

* *Celebrate each tiny step even if it is just sharing your dream with another person or writing it into your journal... Take time to break open the champagne, buy yourself a bouquet of flowers or a new CD or smile at yourself in a mirror with a great beam of self-satisfaction.*

NURTURING THE SEED

Preparing the soil

One of the quickest ways of sabotaging the growth of the seed is to fail to prepare the soil, leaving it barren:

> **"Don't cast your pearls before swine and don't throw your seeds on fallow land."**

To give the seeds the best chance of success, the earth needs to be tilled, weeds and old roots from the previous year's growth need to be removed and healthy nutrients added to the soil. So:

* *What old issues, memories, concerns and dreams are still present in the earth even though their time is over and only their roots remain?*

This is an opportunity to dig up those old roots and release the stagnant energy so it can be used for the new season's growth. Spend a day (or more if needed) in the attic or opening cupboards and unearth those boxes or packages from the past. This includes old love letters, clothes which will never fit again, photos that remind you of memories which prevent you moving forward, and books and lecture notes which you will never read.

* *What ancestral roots are still present in the soil, some of which are highly beneficial bringing with them coping skills for your future, and some of which are stifling your development?*

Roots are important to any growing plant, for without them it will surely die due to inadequate nutrition and support. While preparing the soil it's helpful to examine which ancestral beliefs support your soul's path and which limit it and, as you carefully remove the latter, recognize that they may have been appropriate for their time but not for now.

* *What weeds (outdated or overgrown beliefs) are running wild across the soil preventing the seed from receiving the full impact of the sun?*

By naming and facing our fear, it often brings to light underlying beliefs and helps us to decide if it's time to remove them or whether they still serve us in some way.

* *What would cultivate the growth?*

Commonly we give too little time and space for the seed to grow and then wonder why nothing happened. So making this project a priority, as well as seeking support and backing from the people who love you, goes a long way to enhancing the seed's growth.

* *Aerate the soil by becoming excited and enthusiastic by the project.*

The more excited we are, the more energy we generate from the Universe to help us to see the venture through to the end.

* *What seed did you plant over the past five years that hasn't received your attention for some time…a friendship, marriage, a hobby, or the task of taking care of yourself?*

Sometimes we can happily set a goal but then lose interest or find life taking over, causing us to abandon our precious seed. As the husband said to his wife after he was once again called away at a moment's notice by his employers, *"Well, I have to go as I'm worried that I might lose my job. However, I know you'll still be here when I return."*

"Don't be too sure," she said in exasperation and, when it happened again, she left.

Core values: the natural, organic fertilizers

Our core values are fundamental to inner security and self-respect and are essential for healthy growth. These qualities reflect the energy lines that have flowed through us over lifetimes and that now give us a spiritual integrity against which everything must line up, defining our *inner morality*.

Unfortunately, such morality has been almost abandoned over the years as soul boundaries were adapted to meet our external ego needs and the desires of those who ruled the "tribe", at the cost of true individuality. Because of this, it became necessary to develop external legal and policing services as people could no longer rely on their inner directives to align them to the Universal Laws.

But you only have to listen to the news to see that these modern law makers are losing the battle. Peace and respect for others will not return until we reconnect to spiritual and moral values which are not dictated from outside but emerge from a deep sense of belonging where nothing is hidden and everything is known. Only then will we see a reduction in practices such as sexual, physical or emotional abuse which are allowed to continue practically unabated at the expense of the individual's right to say, *"No!"*

I remember spending time in a small village in Belize, Central America and being told that until recently there had been little crime, for the community spirit was strong with an emphasis on respecting the individual's soul journey. Then drugs permeated the village and the addicts soon lost touch with their own inner morality and self-respect, stealing from neighbors and even from their family to feed the habit. I was clearly shown that punishment did little good, for without self-respect, there was nobody "at home" to be affected. These people had come to understand that it was only by renewing the individual's self-respect and honor within a community that still cared that the addiction could be broken, and that took time and commitment from everybody concerned.

So what are your core values? What do you hold dear to your heart?

These values do not express a judgment towards those who choose to live their life differently but allows everyone to live by qualities that nurture the soul. To test the validity of these values they need to be part of a reciprocal agreement as well as encompass all aspects of the quality,

i.e. *compassion… Can you receive compassion as well as give it? Can you have compassion for yourself even when things are dire?*

Here are others:

* *Honesty…Can you be honest with yourself and can you receive honesty?*

* *Respect…What would you not allow another person to do to you?*

* *Health… What is well-being to you?*

* *Security…What brings you security? What if loved ones have different needs?*

Developing and living by two or three core values strengthens and nourishes the soil in which the seeds are planted, sending out a strong message of our commitment to nurture these impulses until they reach full bloom.

Staying in the center

Once the seed of the idea is planted it acts as a beacon, attracting towards it people and situations that will make it become reality. The more definite we are about our choice to follow this path, the easier it is for the Universe to meet our needs. However, so often we're giving out mixed signals, as I discovered years ago when I thought I was ready to move but subconsciously still had my hand firmly on the brake causing all my efforts to come to nothing.

Frustrated one night, I shouted out to the Universe. *"OK, I give up, I've tried everything,"* and that's when the comment came back, *"That's the problem, stop trying!"* At that my anger turned to laughter as I realized how I was attempting to manipulate every tiny detail. The following morning I received confirmation that I had let go sufficiently to move to the next stage as doors began to open on all levels.

As the Native Americans say: *Trying is Lying;* they believe it suggests that we're not fully motivated by the process and are still holding back through our little self using the throat chakra's willpower to stay in control.

Only when we let go of our little ego and merge with a far deeper intention do we truly understand the awesome nature of the Source.

When I stand in my center, people and events naturally appear to help me to know myself more fully, *all I have to do is turn up!* Now, despite knowing how wonderful it feels to be present and centered, I will admit that in the past I would see myself leaving the center, impatient to get the show on the road, convinced that nothing would happen if I wasn't in control, and failing to trust my own inner guidance. Well, you can imagine the outcome, because when the people and situations that I'd "ordered" arrived, I wasn't "at home" to welcome them!

Staying in the center requires:

* freedom from irrational fears

* deep trust in yourself and the Universe and the ability to be supported by such

* willingness to do the work that will bring you to a place of dynamic readiness

* an understanding that there is a right time and place for everything

* compassion for self and hence others

✳ feet firmly planted on this Earth while our head reaches far into the sky.

And an appreciation that time and space are an illusion, so that Now and Here are the only valuable commodities.

Nowadays, I recognize that when I'm centered and in the flow, important phone calls come through when I'm available, parcels arrive without having to wait in and I have the luxury of experiencing a deep sense of inner peace.

And when I'm in my center, I allow others to be the same.

Here are some helpful tips to encourage nurturing and growth of the seed and movement beyond paralyzing doubts or fears.

✳ *Remember that even though other people may have a similar thought at the same time, like acorns, no two ideas ever appear the same in the end, each growing into its own unique and mighty oak tree.*

✳ *Refrain from impatience which often masks fears of failure or regret; like a pregnant woman, await the inner urgings that signify the natural time for an uncomplicated birth. Observe how the first flowers of Spring wait patiently for the snow to leave before they are prepared to show themselves, whatever the month. Nature recognizes there is no rush as the event will happen at the "right time."*

✳ *Watch for a tendency to change horses half way for something that looks more appealing but which may merely encourage you never to complete any one project. Yes, there will be times when you realize the night-school course you're attending isn't meeting your heart's desires and you decide to make a switch, but recognize where a lack of commitment hides an underlying fear of failure i.e. if I never finish I can never fail.*

* *If you know you need to progress along a certain path but enjoying the experience is difficult, think of a time when you started something that was fun and remember the feelings associated with the event. Now, bring the same enthusiasm to this new venture and observe your change in attitude that allows you to complete the cycle.*

* *Understand there is absolutely no pressure from outside or above to do anything. Only you know whether you'd be left with regret if you failed to follow through on the impulse.*

* *Create a plan and pin it on the wall, allowing each step to be celebrated, rejoicing in the distance you've come rather than looking for how far you still have to go.*

* *Share your idea with someone supportive and who appreciates your fears. Ask them to check in on you at regular intervals but with the understanding that any progress is in your hands and there will be no judgment.*

* *Visualize yourself in a safe space such as the site of a favorite vacation or your own backyard. Find a place to sit and call upon an image of someone who you consider would have no problem in creating and nurturing this idea. This person may be alive or dead or an archetype of courage. Ask them for help and to stand beside you especially when you are challenged by doubts and fears.*

FULL EXPRESSION OF THE IDEA

The well-nourished seedling has given way to a full blooming flower that proudly spreads its petals and turns its face to fully embrace the sun and says, *"Here I am!"* There is no shame or self-judgment for, unlike man, nature doesn't compare itself with others. For some people this is easy: they are the extroverts of the world who love to share their achievements. But for others such exposure is fraught with complications and concerns and they will hold themselves back, standing on the edge of success and fulfillment for fear of judgment or commitment.

We are all endowed with messages passed down through the ages that suggest that to spend too much time thinking of one-self is wrong especially if that time is spent extolling one's own virtues. While we would all have sympathy with such a sentiment after listening for hours to the narcissistic personality whose whole conversation revolves around them, I meet many who have never had the courage to share even minor achievements or blow their own trumpet for fear of comments such as:

Nobody likes a big-head.

You're getting too big for your own good .

What's so special about what you did, anybody could have done that?

Oh, is that all you managed?

No wonder so many fear stepping out and revealing all their beauty and glory; it takes a strong and confident person to celebrate another person's success without seeking something in return. More commonly we encounter those who, unable to experience the full bloom of their own flower, will offer unhelpful advice or comments in response to our efforts, reflecting more than a little of the green-eyed monsters called *envy* and *jealousy*. Many are also concerned that if they expose their innate power and skills then others may reject or abandon them, and hence do everything in their power to keep themselves small. Where rejection is a real possibility I ask you:

Is it better to be abandoned by those who cannot meet you in your true essence, or to reject and abandon yourself for the sake of their possible acceptance and approval?

Building self-worth

Our goal is to seek a place where we neither seek approval or criticism nor are we affected by them, for we recognize and embrace our own essence. The first step is to close the *spigot to your container of self-approval and self-worth* so that when you receive a compliment you allow it to fill and nurture your soul rather than dismiss it with a quick turn of the wrist. As your self-esteem grows you learn whose comments bring sustenance and whose always leave you feeling inadequate. By being able to recognize the difference, it's easier to offer compassion for those who cannot give freely and to establish ways to endorse your own self-worth.

Nobody can make us happy or unhappy; when we fail to believe this, we quickly give our power away.

In the end the choice is ours, for we are the only one who can decide how we wish to live our life, whether through fear or love, remembering that as we celebrate our existence we encourage others to do the same.

So here is an exercise:

Write down four events in your life of which your soul is proud.

These may include:

* *going back to school when you were fifty*

* *learning to drive when you were thirty*

* *taking up swimming when you were forty*

* *staying in a challenging relationship and growing from it*

* *leaving a difficult relationship despite the criticism of others*

* *facing and overcoming an addiction*

* *telling your son to leave when you found him stealing from you, which is true love*

* *building a life for yourself when your partner of many years died*

* *finding a place to love your parent despite all that happened in your earlier life.*

Having made your list, stand tall and read it out to your family, friends or even your dog, allowing yourself to glow with pleasure especially within your heart, for when this fills with joy and appreciation the Universe also smiles. In this way, we celebrate the courage to listen to and follow our intuition, which opened a whole new chapter in our life.

HARVEST AND RELEASE

As the bloom of the petals starts to fade many plants produce fruits that symbolize continuity and connection to the universal web of consciousness. In human terms, the fruit represents wisdom gained through bringing this idea or seed to fruition and indeed is the gem that the soul seeks to enhance its enlightening experience. This is because, during the cycle, light has gone through alchemical transformation passing from wave to particle and then returning to wave again, and this makes the energy, generated and stored in the fruit as wisdom, extremely precious. Wisdom also prevents the soul from continually repeating the same cycle without gaining insight, and moves us to a new level of consciousness. This part of the cycle is symbolized by the Harvest festival celebrated in most ancient traditions, recognizing that as the sun starts to fade from that particular area of the world it stores its light in the fruits and foods. There is commonly feasting for both animals and man, the creation of stores as food for the winter and offerings to the land as nourishment and thanks for its co-operation. As the outer world turns to rest, the soul turns within, taking with it the newly acquired light wisdom and making its inward journey towards the Source.

* * *

So the questions to ask are:

* *How easy is it for you to stop and celebrate the fruits of your endeavors?*

* *Can you take a rest between creative projects, or do you have a tendency to move on to the next one before the last is completed?*

* *Do you feed and nurture those who have worked with you to reach this stage, including aspects of the earth, without which nothing could be achieved?*

* *Are you ready to let go of your achievement so that it might die and eventually allow new seeds to be planted?*

During the menstrual cycle, this phase is represented by an increase in the production of the hormone progesterone, the other important hormone, estrogen being associated with the creative first half of the cycle. Progesterone is the hormone of nurturing and nesting and when levels are low in a woman's cycle she will experience premenstrual syndrome including depression as her body urges her to relax while her mind drives her on, a symptom of modern-day living.

If we consider the heart's rhythm and that the active, contraction phase (systole) is 0.4 seconds long, it often surprises people when I tell them that the relaxation phase (diastole) is exactly the same length, 0.4 seconds, and what is more important is that the heart's muscles receive oxygen during diastole. Is it any wonder that there is a prevalence of heart disease and disorders of the menstrual cycle when individuals work up to 16 hours a day and often find it impossible to switch off even at night. And remember work includes housework and chauffeuring services.

When I mention that treatment involves rest and reflection, I am often met with a look that says, *"You must be joking; I haven't got time to rest, isn't there a tablet I can take?"* Fortunately the body will not always respond to synthetic control and will persist until its message is heard and rest becomes a necessity rather than a luxury.

In this phase of the cycle it is not enough to know you are successful, but to know through literally ingesting the fruits of your success and hence experiencing fulfillment. For some even this is a challenge because it requires them to enjoy the money they've earned, or receive the praise they deserve. But every member of the animal kingdom appreciates the importance of celebration, with many female animals eating the placenta of their young in order to gain nourishment for the next season.

So how do you experience and enjoy the fruits of your endeavors?

Wisdom from patterns

Over the years of my work, I have found that the hardest question to elicit an answer to is:

"So what did you learn from the experience?"

After a look that suggests I asked, *"How many stars are there in the Universe?"* they provide me with a list of beliefs that safely steers the conversation away from them and towards the problems of the world.

"And how did you change because of the experience?" I try again. This is met with further confusion at the absurd idea that events

in their life have anything to do with them or could in any way serve to benefit.

As this phase is so invaluable to the soul, it's certainly helpful to have some conscious appreciation of the wisdom gained from the event even though further insight may not arrive until several years later. In essence, what we seek to achieve is synergy between our original seed and the outcome, between the thought and the result and, hence, come to *know ourselves*. To aid the process we continually repeat the pattern, making subtle adjustments until a match is achieved and we feel an overwhelming sense of coherence and the words, *"Ah-ha,"* slip from our lips.

However, without such insight we often flounder in the dark, often repeating experiences now based on an acquired belief rather than on any rational thought, accompanied by statements that strongly suggest that patterns are forming:

✻ *That always happens to me.*

✻ *That's typical of men/women etc.*

✻ *I never seem to…*

✻ *It's one of my issues.*

At this point it helps to recognize that when we use adverbs such as *always* and *never* we are facing a long-standing belief that is developing resistance to transformation and which could start to act as a stimulus for our actions, stretching across lifetimes, without ever raising one iota of awareness.

For instance when your fourth husband leaves you, or all your nine children refuse to visit, you have to start to see that the problem may not be totally with them but perhaps you have a part to play in the state of affairs. Very often when we acknowledge the deeper significance of the problem and experience the fear that inevitably accompanies it, we naturally feel a shift in consciousness and the next cycle results in a very different ending. At other times we may need professional help to erase the old message and replace it with a new one. But eventually the vibration of the original seed and its fruit will correlate and the cycle will move towards completion as wisdom is gained.

What patterns of belief about money, sex, work etc. may be limiting your soul's expression?

Allowing that which is dead to die

As we complete the harvest, we use our discernment to decide what needs to be stored, what needs to act as compost and what is a weed and needs to be removed and burnt. This is true of our lives especially when we reflect on friendships, beliefs and our physical belongings. This phase is preparing us for completion and death of some part of ourselves, and at this point we need to decide what we will take with us into that place.

* *What friendship is actually dead although you have difficulty accepting the fact?*

* *What belief no longer serves you and needs to be abandoned or transformed so as not to hamper you?*

* *What needs to be cleared so you can enter the void unhampered and explore new depths of possibilities?*

DEATH AND THE CORE CONNECTION

As harvest reaches completion, we enter the final phase of the cycle and turn our attention inwards towards the Winter. For many, who are more comfortable with never-ending activity, this is not seen as a welcome opportunity, often fearing the stillness and emptiness that stretches out before them. And yet, it is essential to retrace our steps to the core of our being and there discharge the wisdom-based light energy that we've collected during our journey and find a still point within the void. If you haven't come to treasure these moments then they can appear as *dark nights of the soul* experienced as a depression or a darkness which descends without warning.

I remember one of my first journeys into the darkness, wondering why I seemed to be the only person affected and really concerned that I was losing my mind. To me it felt as if someone had magically removed the walls, ceiling and floor of my life and I was floating in the nothingness of reality. This experience has repeated itself several times since and I laugh now when I remark that nothing feels real except the ground I'm standing on and I'm not even sure about that! I have learnt to embrace these phases knowing they herald a time of deep reconnection to the Source where I am bathed in the most exquisite, loving, blissful energy.

During such times it's not uncommon to find that those who you thought would support you in this phase are unable to help, often perplexed that you have changed and seem less available to them. I remember that at some of my darkest moments, it has been the stranger who asked if I wanted to talk or who reached out a hand to offer comfort, that made the difference. Many seek solace amongst nature, with animals, in meditation or in their own space, for this is a time of initiation and needs to be treated as such, honoring the deep urges to act or be in a particular way during this phase.

Obviously this can cause its own problems as our busy lives give little opportunity for such self-indulgence. And yet without it we find ourselves completely out of alignment with our soul's rhythm, resulting in illnesses such as depression, heart disease, diseases of the immune system (including fibromyalgia and cancer) and endocrine illnesses such as hypothyroidism, diabetes and menstrual disorders. These diseases are not the cause of the problem but the signs of someone who is desperately seeking a reconnection to their soul and ultimately to the Source and doesn't know another way to make it happen.

Imagine preventing an animal from its usual pattern of hibernation or a plant from dying back in the winter; it would be similar to trying to stop the mighty tides or preventing the sun from setting in the evening. To the soul such a lack of connection and remembering is devastating and drains the life force until there is only a shell present. Medication can help us to see there is a problem and lift us to a place from which we can act, but it's not the answer. What the soul needs is support and encouragement to follow its intuition and enter the void for vital spiritual renewal.

If you have ever been present during a death, you'll have noticed the stillness that immediately descends when we stop fighting and surrender to the inevitable. To many such loss of control is terrifying and they will hold on with their last ounce of energy, attempting to defy death with the latest medical breakthroughs. But if we truly understand that our physical body is simply a *cloak* we drop as we move into a richer reality, we would embrace death and not perceive it as a failing.

I can only imagine that when the spirit world views our attempts to maintain physical form at the expense of our soul life, they must sigh, especially at a time when we are moving away from manifestation and into dematerialization. Why would we wish to remain in our junior school when far more opportunities are being offered in a senior college? Why would the caterpillar refuse the cocoon when it knew that the butterfly was waiting to emerge? Over the next few years as Uranus and Neptune move through Pisces we will witness the collapse of many institutions that have caused us to believe that they can offer physical, structural and financial security as a means of defying death.

Fortunately death is inevitable, what remains in our hands is how we chose to live our lives.

Whether death is physical or psycho-spiritual, as we accept the cup we fall into the void or the place of emptiness. Here we enter the Cauldron or womb of the Great Mother where water, fire and air meet and our previous structure is broken down allowing our spirit freedom. We become the *Phoenix*, the mythical bird whose name means *red gold* and who when burnt to ashes, transforms into *white gold*, the ultimate aim of alchemical practice.

It is here we meet the three *wyrd* or *weird* sisters, or the three wise men depending on the culture, who review our life's path and measure our soul's worth. This trinity will decide the fate by examining the purity of our hearts and how authentic or true to our soul's frequency have we lived our lives. But prior to this we are held suspended in the place of *being*, the gap, the place between breaths between words, between activity: *stillness*.

And here we remain between time and space for a metaphorical three to three-and-a-half days recorded in the teachings of many spiritual disciplines, symbolizing the trinity of experiences (birth, bloom and release) and the half day of transcendent consciousness. The Tibetan's book of the *Living and the Dead*, stresses how important it is to sit with the body during this time of soul transition, comparable to the women waiting at the tomb of Jesus. Even in modern science we know that it takes three days for the DNA to respond to a new messenger and so it is with us.

Then, from nowhere, we become conscious of a powerful flow of energy as if we were looking down on a river of molten lava, miles below. Despite the distance, we feel the movement within our being and recognize that it has always been there, but it's only in the stillness that we appreciate its presence. This is *Shakti*: pure, feminine, creative energy, the nectar of life. Into this, with the help of the wyrd sisters, we will cast our fishing line of intention and draw on her power until we are once again reborn.

This place is known to every woman, for each month during menstruation, she enters the void and taps into this immense power of the feminine before emerging newly born. This is why many ancient cultures prohibit menstruating women from their ceremonies for they consider them too powerful at this time, linked as they are to shakti energy.

* * *

And so we return from our journey into the Great Mother having surrendered ourselves for the opportunity to experience her trinity: the void, the elixir of creative power and her powerful breath which expels us back out into the world to commence the next cycle.

So are you ready to surrender and hence experience yourself in a manner that will truly take your breath away and give you a new meaning to life?

Healing the Family Tree

The completion of the cycle, where intention and reality meet, causes us to ascend the spiral of awareness to a new frequency of consciousness. However, there are many times when the end result does not equate to the intention, and instead of creating a flowing spiral we create a fixed *knot*. If this were present within a string instrument, we would certainly hear disharmony. However, our purpose is to know ourselves more fully and hence where there is a knot (folded petal). Then we are given ample opportunities in this and subsequent lives to refine our perceptions and our process and eventually achieve a satisfactory result.

Now imagine you are not the only person in your family who has attempted to clear this line but that, when you look at those who are trapped by the knot, you recognize many familiar faces who are unable to grow spiritually until someone succeeds in completing the cycle. Hence you are being presented with the opportunity to not only help yourself but release all those caught in this particular strand of the web, raising consciousness for all concerned.

Here is the important part of the story to know:

The knot is not the problem, it is the answer.

The knot provides us with a *keyhole* or *portal* into our next level of awareness, because the original essence of the knot was an impulse of energy which, had it reached its goal, would have increased the frequency of the line. It therefore still contains this new vibration and is awaiting fulfillment rather than destruction. I believe this to be true for the majority of illnesses we see today, which are often perceived as the problem whereas, in my experience, they are the solution. If we can hear and understand their message, perhaps through the use of voice dialogue, we can then find the solution rather than "kill the messenger".

Joanne was a six-year old in a family where the motto was "harmony at any cost" which worked, except that it commonly prevented honest communication between the family members. When Joanne was diagnosed as hyperactive, the family immediately identified her as the one with the problem and sought a quick fix. However, a wise healthcare practitioner recognized the deeper problem and that Joanne was merely acting out the disharmony which came from years of unexpressed emotions on a collective level.

It became clear that Joanne was sending out a new frequency of behavior which, although rather untamed, started to entrain the rest of the family to express their deeper emotions and frustrations and began a whole new dynamic of family life. (Entrainment occurs when two tuning forks of the same frequency are brought together and the one that is vibrating causes the one that is still to start to vibrate.)

This is the principle behind homeopathy and acupuncture, where the symptoms provide the therapist with the ability to see what needs healing, i.e. what will bring the individual to a state of wholeness. In homoeopathy, where energetically based substances are used, we recognize that the symptoms are merely an outer representation of the energy which is awaiting birth, and choose a remedy that mirrors the symptoms. In this way, we offer the body a stronger representation of the frequency that is present in the knot. Then, through the process of entrainment, the remedy encourages the vibration of the knot to awaken, causing it to unwind and transform the energy line.

I have witnessed powerful healers achieve the same result by offering their own stronger vibration to release the knot, although it becomes more meaningful to the soul when we untie the knot through our own endeavors. By looking at recurrent patterns, habits or illnesses in your family tree you can identify the knots of awareness which are awaiting your focus. If we study heart disease for instance, we meet a group of people who often describe being trapped in a cul-de-sac with no way out and where joy and freedom have deserted them. Despite being surrounded by a loving family they commonly experience feelings of isolation and are experts at denying their deeper feelings preferring to keep silent or busy.

Rather than seeing a problem, it helps to appreciate that the illness is offering the opportunity to change patterns of perception which have plagued many generations in the past. *Simon came from such a family where all the men in his family died early with heart disease. On a psychological level, there was a pattern of dedication to professional success at the expense of outside happiness. Unfortunately, in this particular case, most of the men ended up hitting a ceiling to further advancement and without the means to find joy elsewhere. By absorbing the lessons from his family, he understood the pressure and fears of his ancestors and appreciated their motto of "pride in achievement" which was his heritage. However, he saw achievement on a far wider scale which included family life and inner fulfillment. He therefore vowed at the age of thirty-five that, whatever happened, he would not allow himself to reach such a cul-de-sac in his work, making sure that he took ample time to be with the family. Now retired and watching his grandchildren play, he has no regrets and knows that he has reprogrammed the heart energy line for his family and perhaps for many other people.*

Healing of the family tree asks that we are willing to:

1. Turn and face what is uncomfortable rather than seeking to fix it through medication, deny its presence or blame it on someone else. Sixty per cent of healing occurs through honest awareness.

2. Appreciate if possible the aspect of the soul that is being presented rather than merely concentrating on the disease, i.e. *is this about compassion, honesty, truth, etc.?*

3. Explore that issue within yourself and engage the part of you that holds such a memory moving through fears, shame, etc. that often surround such a knotty problem.

4. Radiate love from your heart into this aspect of the self and feel its integration into your soul. Such love is not from pity or judgment but as a parent who loves all their children equally recognizing that each is a part of the whole.

One last observation I want to share is that I have met some people who seem to hit the jackpot when it comes to issues they are facing in this life. Some may say it's their karma or that they are a new soul and hence the struggles. But my impression is that these people are highly evolved souls who have chosen to come onto this planet to clear as many energy lines as possible and hence lift the vibration of humanity to a new level so that we may experience the energetic web of Christ Consciousness.

✳ ✳ ✳

Working with the Labyrinth

Labyrinths are associated with most ancient cultures painted on rocks, carved into stone, laid out in the Earth, weaved into baskets or created through plants. They were used at times of death and rebirth, initiation, fertility and as a spiritual journey. Different from a maze with its dead ends and frustration, a labyrinth is unicursal with only one way in and out and with the center always visible wherever you are in its coherent circuits. Since the route is guaranteed, the journey can be carried out in meditation and silence allowing for contemplation and transformation.

Labyrinths represent the spiral of creativity with the center being the place of death and rebirth. Nowadays, these ancient geometric forms are appearing in many different locations around the world as well as in hospitals, retreats and in private homes. Even small, finger labyrinths are being drawn and used in the home or office.

Wherever they are found they usually consist of one of two forms. The first is Cretan dating back 3,500 years with its seven circuits and associated with the Minotaur's journey, and the other is found on the floor of Chartres Cathedral created in the 13th century by the Knight's Templars. The latter has 11 concentric circles that wind through four quadrants of the encompassing circle with a rosette of six petals in its center representing the rose of the Virgin Mary. This closely resembles the six circles of the "seed of life" surrounding the one circle with the petals representing the "birth of life."

The Chartres Labyrinth

What can labyrinths do?

* Deepen spirituality by taking one inward and connecting
  to the soul

* Enhance access to intuition and creativity

* Expand integration of body and soul, balancing left and
  right hemispheres

* Allow us to switch off from the outer world and develop
  a rhythm of the soul, outside labels and roles

* Help to deepen the connection in relationships and
  the community

There is no right or wrong way of working with the labyrinth
and the journey is as important as the goal. But you may enjoy
finger-walking the labyrinth, printed here, experimenting with your
dominant and non-dominant hands, with a variety of intentions
which include:

a) The center representing birth and asking the questions:

What am I ready to give birth to?

What fears may arise to prevent this?

How will I feel when I succeed in reaching the center?

b) The center representing death and asking the questions:

What needs to be allowed to die in my life?

What may prevent me surrendering to the inevitable?

What feelings arise when I reach the center?

The Cretan Labyrinth

Chapter Three

Alchemy: The Marriage of Opposites

The Philosopher's stone

The Count Saint Germain was one of the best-known alchemists within the last 500 years. A confidant of kings and a friend to those in power, he could truly turn base metals into gold but that was not all. He knew this to be a spiritual experience. Born in the late part of the 17th century, he remained youthful 100 years on, advising the French, Dutch and English courts and playing a major role in the foundation of the United States of America. He described alchemy as such:

> *The inner meaning of alchemy is simply all-composition, implying the relation of all of creation with the parts which compose it. Thus alchemy, when properly understood, deals with the conscious power of controlling mutations and transmutations within Matter and energy and even within life itself. It is the science of the mystic and the forte of self-realized man who, having*

> *sought, has found himself to be one with God and is*
> *willing to play his part.*
>
> **Saint Germain** *(Saint Germain on Alchemy)*

Anyone who has heard of alchemy, knows of the philosopher's stone, the catalyst used to turn base metal into gold. Many have sought to find such a treasure and hence to become rich, however its identity is shrouded in mystery. It has been described in paradoxical terms as, *"a Stone which is not a stone, with origins which are both divine and earthly and made from a substance which is enormously expensive and yet is regarded as worthless."*

When we look deeper, we find that perhaps the philosopher's stone didn't turn base metal into gold, but was gold itself, as described by researcher and historian, Laurence Gardner, who talks of a weightless, high-spin gold being produced through the use of an arc light. Historical texts show that by ingesting this substance an alchemical process occurred through the stimulation of the pineal gland, leading to extended life and probable transcendent experiences.

Other studies have looked for a more esoteric approach to achieve the same result as the gold and suggest that this Stone consists of the conjunction of opposites such as between *Fire and Water, when the Red Lion marries the White Queen, the Sun marries the Moon, or the dragon enters the womb of the Mother while the father copulates with the daughter.*

Jung concurred with this hypothesis stating that alchemical symbolism expressed what he called *individuation* which was the marriage of opposites in a union that transcends the contraries. The existence of opposites and their intrinsic duality is considered to be the source of all change and creativity but also the source of many of our sorrows and suffering. In the 1800s, Georg Hegel introduced the *dialectical method* based on the means by which Greek philosophers, such as Socrates, settled philosophical disputes by successive contradictions. A *thesis* would be suggested which would be met by the opposing side's *antithesis* until, in the course of the argument, a *synthesis* was reached in which the conflicting ideas were resolved. From this we could suppose that the marriage of opposites hopes to result in a synthesis.

However, Jung is suggesting something far more transformational and radical by saying that our final aim is not synthesis but emancipation from polarity creating the One from which new worlds will evolve. Many spiritual practices aim to achieve such a goal, especially those which involve *Tantra* found within Jainism, Hinduism and Buddhism. For the most part, Tantra has been known for its sexual practices although it is a far wider discipline than this, incorporating meditation, yoga and sacramental worship in a technique of spiritual action, with the main aim being to take the individual to new levels of consciousness.

In terms of Hindu Tantra, the negative element of polarity is regarded as male and is known as *Shiva*, while the feminine, dynamic element is known as *Shakti*. Together they exist within everything that has life, from viruses to archangels. In humanity, Shakti energy is symbolized by the serpent, the kundalini, which, in the unenlightened, is curled up, sleeping at the base of the spine. There are many techniques to awaken the slumbering serpent so that she might rouse herself and ascend the spine along the subtle energy pathways until unity is achieved with Shiva, who lives above the Crown of the head.

This divine marriage of opposing polarities is then believed to destroy inner duality and liberate the tantric initiate from pain, suffering and the modalities of time and space.

In essence this is the path of our journey: the ability to create unity through conscious awareness of opposites and eventually through their sacred marriage. Every aspect of the self with which we engage during the creative cycle has its opposite which needs to be acknowledged, experienced and integrated.

Each time we cross the central point or the node, the energy we have accumulated enters the pool of light energy also known as Shakti. The further we are willing to travel from the center in either direction to know ourselves, the greater the amount of energy or wisdom we will return to the core. If through fear we never live further than 15 miles from the home in which we were born, it is hard for us to say that we understand the world. We do not seek balance but rather stability around a central fulcrum similar to two people sitting on the ends of a see-saw rather than one standing in the middle where the opposing forces do not apply. It takes courage to step out and take a risk especially into the unknown parts of ourselves. But without this the serpent cannot rise, for it requires the energy generated by movement around the creative cycle to make its journey.

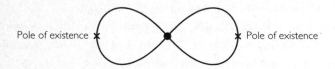

Pole of existence ✗   ✗ Pole of existence

So to reiterate: to know ourselves is to express ourselves fully in both poles of existence, extending the range to its furthest effect. For example, *if you know love, do you know hate and if you are always "good" is there any badness anywhere within your being?* As we come to accept and draw these parts into our heart, the flow of energy starts to merge. We see that these so called differences are merely two sides of the same coin and like the yin and yang signs are reciprocally supportive, continuously giving birth to each other.

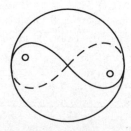

As the flow increases and the two sides meet in the place of *forgiveness and compassion*, increasing levels of light energy in the form of consciousness are produced and enter the core of our being.

Meeting the shadow

So now let us explore this theory in terms of our own patterns of life:

"Where are you placing emphasis on one side of the dynamic while ignoring the other, causing instability?"

Marina recognized that she had achieved top marks and gold stars for her responsible nature, written up in report cards from the age of five and enhanced during her years in a caring profession. For a long time, she saw nothing wrong with this and reveled in the pride that her job gave her. But slowly and with some reluctance she recognized the following:

* *She inwardly resented and judged those who took life and duty far less seriously than she did.*

* *Through her heightened sense of responsibility, she often denied others the opportunity to be responsible for themselves thereby surreptitiously maintaining control over them.*

* *She was lousy at being responsible for her own nurturing, preferring to deny herself the pleasure in the name of martyrdom, waiting for someone else to rescue her and then refusing their help!*

* *She found being irresponsible very challenging especially if she believed that someone else may suffer as a consequence. Hence she consistently gathered around her people who subtly implied that if she was happy while they were suffering, she was being irresponsible!*

✳ *Her ego arrogantly believed that she was ultimately
responsible for the destiny of others.*

I offer Marina's list of honest confessions to trigger the reader's
own understanding of how a perfectly appropriate action can
turn into a nightmare of delusions, dramas and coping mechanisms, nearly all of which are mainly fear driven. At the same
time, there was an empty circle of awareness awaiting her called
spontaneity and fun and thankfully she chose that path and never
looked back.

However, if we don't accept and integrate our opposite pole then we will marry it!

How many times do I hear "responsible" members of society
become extremely irate at their partner, who appears to have no
idea about time keeping, organizing files, nor a sense of duty. Such
partnerships can work very well with each supplying the other
with a purpose for being in the relationship. However, as Marina
found, there comes a time when being the strong, capable one
who has all the answers starts to wear thin and resentment sets
in. Of course, not everybody wants you to give up the familiar
role and will attempt to send you on a guilt trip with words such
as, *"I thought you were strong, available, responsible, spiritual, caring etc. It's not like you."* Which is really saying, *"Don't change
as I might have to do the same!"* But there comes a point in all our
lives when it is not possible to improve on a skill and extra activity in that direction only serves to dilute its effectiveness.

So I ask you, *"What talent or gift can you no longer learn or
grow from?"*

*"What quality within you, which you excel at, is no longer nur-
turing your soul?"*

It is not that you have to abandon your gift of caring but rather
examine the opposite pole and find stability around the central

point. So commonly, we find it easier to ignore the inner signals of resentment, lack of enthusiasm, exhaustion or despair, as we have invested so much energy in our performance that we are reluctant to let go of its security, even though it may kill us. And then there is the fear of the unknown, the opposite pole, waiting for us to enter and we don't even know the code word. Yet, without this journey across the center to this new aspect of ourselves, we fail to bring further light consciousness to our soul which will slowly start to disconnect.

Some people will be forced to the other side due to a crisis such as illness, while others will go more willingly, seeing the virtues it holds. When we can see that we would experience pleasure, joy and nurturing from entering the other pole we are far more likely to move than when we see only pain.

Here are a few suggestions to help make the move:

1. Write a list of all the positive values that you could derive from such a shift, and imagine experiencing each of them, sensing the response in your body and especially within the heart.

2. Imagine there is a part of you that has already passed through the doorway into the other polarity and is encouraging you to make the journey. Dialogue with that part until your confidence grows.

3. Recognize where you may be limiting others by holding your position, i.e. they cannot or need not become responsible while you are there as superman/woman.

4. Create affirmations that fill you with good feelings: *"I feel my whole body glow when I take care of myself,"* or, *"I get great pleasure when watching others become more confident as I step back."*

Mirrors of awareness

If we are unsure of the poles of existence that await us, we just have to look around and the world supplies us with a myriad of opportunities for reflection. A valuable exercise is to walk down a stretch of road and write down three things that catch your attention within 20 minutes, whether visual, auditory, kinesthetic or as an aroma. I have found that, despite the fact that a number of us may perform the same exercise, we will all be drawn to specific areas that stimulate our own holographic memory.

Obviously, those things that reflect a fully opened aspect of ourselves may almost go unnoticed apart from a sense of reassurance as it resonates with our being. However, we may also be attracted to images that reveal an area of our life that requires attention, and we know this to be true by the level of emotion associated with the event. Hence, when we overreact to something we've heard and everybody else is unaffected, then we need to own the stimulus, remembering that there are many positive parts of ourselves awaiting rediscovery and mirrors are not always negative.

Other than events or objects in our environment, there will also be people who willingly join us on some stages of our journey so that we might see a part of ourselves reflected in them. This may be someone whom you greatly admire and wish to emulate or someone who drives you crazy...they are both soul friends!

For instance:

* *the woman whose beauty causes you to look twice*

* *the woman who is always so critical*

* *the man who can make a room come alive just with his presence*

* *the woman who has such confidence when speaking in public*

* *the man who always speaks before he engages his brain*

* *the man whose demeanor makes you feel strong and safe in his company.*

What is important is to remember that not everyone provides us with a simple mirror but may be revealing a part that needs to act in a different way. Hence:

* *The woman who is always so critical **may be** showing you your critical nature or **may be** encouraging you to stop fading in her presence and share your feelings on the matter.*

* *The woman who has such confidence when speaking in public **may be** telling you that you could do the same or **may be** helping you to have the confidence to decline that lecture engagement because you really don't like speaking in public!*

* *The man who speaks before he engages his brain **may be** mirroring your tendency to do the same or **may be** helping you to move beyond your tendency to analyze everything before you speak, and just let rip!*

I want to mention one other situation I have observed and that is when someone, especially a member of the family, chooses to hold one side of the polarity for you, so that you can experience the other side. Hence, what is known as the "black sheep of the family" may actually be the shepherd who is guiding everybody towards a greater, inner light. So when you look at someone who perhaps you judge for their way of life, ask whether they may in fact be providing an invaluable service.

* * *

Here is one final suggestion you might wish to employ if you haven't discovered why someone is in your life. Next time you are together, go up to them and say, *"You know, you really annoy me but I know you have something that I need to appreciate so that I can become a more integrated individual. Please help me to see what it is so we can both get on with our lives!"*

* * *

Consciousness asks that we should know ourselves in all aspects of the Truth, and will attempt to show us where we are limited for, in essence, there is no *right or wrong* or *good or bad*, for everything is part of the Divine. Whenever we judge we limit our soul's growth and our ultimate potential, for it's only through the knowledge of the whole can we find the place of discernment which sits within the third eye. And such knowledge is not found within books but within our own experiences or the experiences of those we care about.

Stan thought he was a good doctor, having built up a practice with clients who respected him for his level of compassion and tolerance. He enjoyed working with young people, especially the men, where he felt he could provide a solid support which was often lacking in their own homes.

Then one day he learnt that his 15-year-old son was taking drugs, and he hit the roof. For days he ranted at his son telling him how disappointed he was and that he would find it very difficult to forgive. Despite the fact that he offered a listening ear and advice to others, he couldn't do the same for his son. In time, he slowly understood that he only played lip service to the reasons why young people took drugs because he saw it as someone else's problem; now it was his own.

As father and son created a whole new relationship around honesty and tolerance, Stan's healing approach took on a completely new depth.

As the native Americans say: "Walk a mile in someone's moccasins before you say you understand."

* *Can you love the saint and sinner?*

* *Can you love yourself not only when things are going well but also on the days you would rather forget?*

The most important part of the agenda is the willingness to see all parts of ourselves in the mirror and find a place of acceptance:

* *If you are generous person can you ever be penny-pinching?*

* *If you are always in control, does it hide a fear of insecurity?*

* *If you know you're intelligent, who can make you feel stupid?*

* *If you have a deep love for people, have you felt hate to protect that love?*

* *If you are a good person, do you inwardly judge those who fall short?*

Forgiveness

I believe it's only by experiencing ourselves at the poles and finding a place of love and acceptance for both that we start to draw the energy between the poles together in the name of *forgiveness*.

Forgiveness is not a passive, mental exercise completed before you have a true understanding of the situation but rather the conclusion of an event after going through powerful emotions and accepting our soul's part in creating the scenario in the first place. From a spiritual point of view, true forgiveness is the result of recognizing there is no separation between ourselves and the person who has offended, for we are all one. While we maintain any separation we cannot achieve true forgiveness, for the word clearly states that we should be able to *give first* and that in my mind means releasing the boundaries and finding space in the heart for acceptance.

It asks us to have the courage to travel into the depths of consciousness and find that part that waits alone, bringing it into our heart so we might love it unconditionally without the need to understand with our heads but only with our hearts. In this place there is no judgment or emotional attachment to the result but merely the willingness to accept another level of consciousness and offer this up to the Universe.

Chapter Four

Stepping into the Hologram

CITIES OF ENERGY

It is not only people who carry a vibration that attracts our attention but also places. Remember visiting somewhere for the first time where you felt so much at home there was little need for a map or translation skills. Some may say this was due to a past-life memory, which is certainly possible, but perhaps the memory is more deeply related to an association with an energy rather than just the experience.

The question to ask is:

What quality is being evoked through engaging with this place?

My own experience of this occurred many years ago during one of my first visits to New York where I found myself becoming physically unbalanced by the powerful energy that ran through the city. My inner guidance advised me to seek some granite, and the following morning at sunrise I found myself standing on a rock in Central Park, fairly inconspicuous to the intense concentration of joggers, dog walkers and those on their way to work. As I stood there, I heard my inner voice suggest that I should ask to meet an angel and, although not particularly versed in angels, found myself following the advice and receiving a resounding and almost instantaneous response, *"North or South?"* Recovering my stance on the rock, I asked, *"Well, who are you?"*

"North," the voice continued with an intensity similar to the people who busily moved around me as the sun's rays started to cut across the city. *"What would you like to say?"* I asked, still a little wary of the assertive manner of my new friend.

"Don't think that the people here are so active without my help. They are motivated by my energy and not the other way round. What you have to decide is whether this is the energy for you?"

That was the first time I really came to understand that every city and country holds its own frequency of energy. This is not due to the people but to the web of energy lines, often known as an Angelic presence, that passes through the location causing the rise or fall in disease rates, which is observed when families move from one place to another.

Our behavior, mannerisms, biases and pleasures are influenced by the Earth's own energetic memory, i.e. its consciousness, with different facets appearing in different parts of the world.

Can we influence that memory?

Yes, because it is just consciousness, although most of the time our thoughts are so scattered and fear-driven that they are like a fly's irritating hum to this more powerful and concentrated force. Fear will always limit our ability to raise our consciousness to a level where we can make a difference. As you will see later, our aim as an alchemist is to clear our own paths of energy from dysfunctional emotions and beliefs and thereby liberate the full potential of our force and focus so that we can truly become co-creators of our reality.

The ability to feel in resonance with certain parts of the world is highlighted in the practice of *astrocartography* which places your natal astrology chart on the world's map and outlines what personal qualities you will tap into when visiting specific areas. For instance, on my chart, Mars, the planet of action, assertion and masculinity, runs through New York stimulating and exciting my male side but doing little for my feminine essence. That is probably the reason why I thoroughly enjoy visiting New York at regular intervals but presently live happily in Southern California!

Webs of energy

On a more global level we are gifted with ancient sites scattered around the world which have been the seat of meetings, worship and sacred practice for thousands of years. During a recent visit to the beautiful and at least 5,000-year-old site of Newgrange in Southern Ireland, I came to appreciate that the spirit people who originally designed this site saw it as a place where the vibrations of heaven and earth literally could meet and marry: *As above so below.* Like many other places, its unique location, geometric dimensions and the chemical configuration of the material used as building blocks, provide a distinct vibration for this meeting, especially at certain times in the year such as the solstices and the equinoxes.

I came to understand that these sites were not necessarily built for human initiation but to maintain energetic flow between the *grids* or *webs of consciousness* that encircle our planet and are part of a far greater network forming what we know as the Universe. The grid that is seeking our attention at present is related to Christ Consciousness, or unity consciousness, and is shaped as a dodecahedron (12 equal five-sided faces). But inside this grid are others connected to lower levels of consciousness that are constantly being fed by our instincts, emotions and beliefs.

If you understand that our physical body has an aura consisting of multiple subtle energy bodies, so it is with the Earth and with the Universe. Remember looking at a spider's web and seeing concentric circles that are linked by radial strands that start from the center and move out to the edge.

Spider's Web

We could say that the Universal web consists of concentric circles (although they often take on other shapes) linked to:

1. The *etheric body*, associated with all electromagnetic energy of the Earth including the physical body and also known as ley lines: *third dimension*

2. The *astral or emotional body*, associated with the emotional body and accessed through the feelings and the psychic senses: *fourth dimension*

3. *The mental body*, associated with beliefs, thoughts and willpower: *fifth dimension*

4. The *soul body*, associated with soul consciousness and the intuition; the Christ Consciousness grid: *sixth dimension*.

5. *The spiritual body*, associated with our Higher Self and its link to all aspects of spirit: *seventh dimension*

6. *The universal or divine body*, associated with the state of union with the Source: *eighth dimension*, and the start of a new octave.

It is interesting to note that the spider is able to move without becoming tangled in its own web, because the lines that run radially are not sticky, only those that are concentric. In other words, we experience non-locality, freedom and a multi-dimensional reality when we move out from our center and a local or manifested reality when we walk along the concentric lines. Hence, we can move between chaos and structure, timelessness and time, all of which are vital if we are to experience the full consciousness of the web.

These multi-dimensional webs were set in place at the beginning of time, but the polarity of flow has changed many times through the Ages, often by the hand of man, when men were still "gods" and understood the holographic principle of creation.

In simple terms, the webs hold an energy field that causes the manifestation of what we perceive as reality but in truth is a holographic image. The purpose of the sacred site is to act as a lightning rod, maintaining flow, transmitting information and transforming energy when the consciousness of the web changes. In terms of the Christ Consciousness Grid, the main areas concerned are the west coast of the Americas, Egypt, Israel, Greece and the Himalayas and include the Egyptian pyramids, Palenque in Mexico, Tikal in Guatemala, Lake Titicaca in Peru and sites in parts of California and Hawaii. We also know that at certain times, especially during Atlantis, crystals were placed both above and below our planet to alter and strengthen the holographic image so that it created a more solid reality and hence provide greater satisfaction to our five physical senses.

We exist in a holographic Universe which means that it's as real as our mind perceives it to be. If you believe it, there is the potential to create it.

I want you to understand that the creation of the hologram, elaborated upon later, is the way in which we manifest our reality all the time. Nothing is solid except within our minds which, along with the collective mind, has agreed to believe in the dense nature of our planet. At some level, a long time ago, we all agreed to utilize the holographic approach to create reality, including the formation of our own physical body, as we wanted to see the extent of our alchemical talents. However, slowly we became entranced by our creations and failed to remember that we were involved in the *great experiment*, preferring to fall asleep to a deeper intention. Over time, the reality, which was in truth pure illusion, became fixed in our minds and the so-called spiritual world became the place of fantasy to be visited only during dreams or meditation.

New holographic images are being produced all the time in response to collective awareness which can transform any idea into fact when enough people believe it and hence the hundredth monkey effect. You only have to travel from one country to the next to see where one man's myth is another man's reason. I will be listening to someone tell me something that is very valid to them and, because it fails to fit into my understanding of the world, I want to shout out, *"You must be kidding,"* and then see they're not! Who's wrong? Neither, it's just that we have different experiences and perceptions and hence what, for them is undeniable, I record as a *"maybe"*.

I was told this story by a woman who had traveled in a so-called developing area in Asia where she found herself surrounded by poverty and dirty-faced children milling around their mothers. She was about to offer help from a place of pity when one of the women said in broken English, *"It must be very sad to be a mother in your country, for we hear that from early morning to late in the day, you have to give your children into the care of strangers because you need to leave the house to work. You have our sympathy."*

Our cultural realities and hence our holographic productions are largely dependent on what we've been taught to believe, leaving a loophole for anyone who wishes to exploit the situation for financial advantage or self-gain.

If you can persuade enough people to believe something, then

it will eventually take form and nobody will ever remember or question who expressed the original idea.

But times are changing and we are no longer moving into greater manifestation but into dissolving. This has become more and more apparent to me as I visit sacred parts of the world such as Cusco in Peru, Ephesus in Turkey or the Olgas in the outback of Australia, where the veil between the dimensions is thin. By softening my eyes (defocusing) I can see the most "dense" holographic image shimmer as the reality starts to dissipate before my eyes and I catch a glimpse of what lies beyond this particular holographic façade.

During this time of the Great Shift, there will be increasing distortion of the hologram as individuals reconnect to their own divine consciousness and choose not to follow a collective truth unless it resonates with their soul. As we clear our perceptions and filters, it will become increasingly easy to see "right through" structures or ideas that have no deep spiritual substance and fail to emit the unifying vibration of love. We will only be able to "see" those things that resonate with our soul's memory, for it is this inner knowing that will bring alive the holographic representation of the Christ Consciousness Grid.

We see the hologram because we hold the memory of its image within our soul's cellular light memory.

Of course, we will continue to create holographic images, but I perceive that the new paradigm of reality will consist of *diversity within a unified field* and hence will be multi-dimensional and interconnected. Whatever you wish to believe, you will perceive and live within, expanding the scope of consciousness to meet the planet's needs while allowing the individual to maintain their sense of free will. Other distortions to the holographic field will also occur over the next few years due to new energies that are arriving on this planet from higher dimensions, aimed at assisting us to remember a deeper reality. This may come in ways that shock us from our complacency, but with Uranus (the planet of sudden change) moving into Pisces (the sign of illusion) from

March 2003, I would say expect the unexpected and be prepared to let go of the way you've seen the world in the past.

THE HOLOGRAPHIC UNIVERSE

The idea that we and the world we live in exist because of the meeting of beams of light or consciousness, opens the door to an exploration of holographic formations. My own interest in this subject was stimulated many decades ago when visiting an exhibition promoting communication technology. As I wandered around the various stands, my attention was drawn to an area completely surrounded with visitors. Squeezing through the crowds to see what was attracting so much interest, I was amazed to find myself almost face to face with a hologram, an image of a man selling the company's most innovative product: himself.

I stood entranced for almost 20 minutes, not only respecting the skills used to produce such a perfect representation of human movements and physical demeanor, but because this image, which I could easily walk through, felt and looked so real. My left brain was scrambling to find answers and to reprogram its previous knowledge on reality, while my right brain knew its importance and relevance to my future.

Since then we've experienced *holodecks* and *medical holograms* in the Star Trek adventures, and many businesses are using holograms on business cards or during their presentations. However, I want to bend your mind enough to help you to realize the hologram is not outside us but is *who we are*: a product of the meeting of light beams which creates the illusion called *matter*. Stay with me on this as I describe how a hologram is produced and relate it to the subject at hand: the creation of reality. For it is *time to remember* that **we are** a holographic universe, a microcosm of the macrocosm.

In order to create a hologram, a beam of coherent light, a laser, is split by a beam splitter with one beam being sent to the object to be photographed and then onto the photographic plate, and the other, the reference beam, reflected off a mirror and then onto the plate. Where the two beams meet they create an *interference pattern* which can be likened to ripples of water meeting when two separate stones are thrown into the pond.

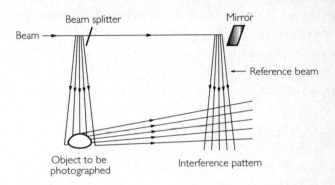

What is important to understand is that when we look at the interference pattern itself, it is not possible to see the object that was photographed, for all you see are the ripples or the matrix, the coded blueprint. It is only when another beam of laser light is shone onto the interference pattern that the original object is revealed and appears to occupy our 3D world unlike the 2D pictures we reproduce using an ordinary camera.

Interference Pattern + Laser Light = Hologram

Now there are other factors that are important in bringing the image *alive*:

* The angle at which the second laser light shines upon the photographic plate will enhance or decrease the clarity of the image, remembering how you have to move the holographic card in your hand to see the image clearly.

* The specific angle used will dictate which aspects of the object you will observe.

* The three-D holographic image can also be seen when a separate image of the same object is projected onto the interference pattern.

Interference Pattern + Same Image = Hologram

When forming the image of the salesman, the holographic producers created the perfect angle and laser light to create a reproduction that appeared authentic. However, as alchemical apprentices, we are still developing our holographic skills and therefore we often reach the stage of the interference pattern and then are unable to bring the holograph alive. In the same way, our own holographic image is still developing as we continue to align our soul's intention with our manifested self. As the process of *seeing ourselves in different lights* continues, consciousness expands and our hologram comes alive.

The ability to be seen in our full holographic form is directly proportional to the light energy we have generated through the various cycles of creativity. The more coherent the light, that is, the more that we know of ourselves in all our facets, the more able this light can shine on our own interference pattern, bringing our hologram into awareness and allowing everybody to see us in our "true" light. *This is enlightenment.*

Let us look at how we can develop a more coherent light. The original beam is the undifferentiated, pure light or ocean of consciousness (chaos). The beam splitter is my intention, i.e. where I choose to place my attention and the force I apply to such a decision. *"I want (force) to enhance my self-worth (focus),"* which is often a relatively unconscious choice. Once the beam is split, the reference beam, carrying the memory of the original intention, is first reflected off a mirror before entering the photographic plate. The other beam is sent through the filters of our perceptions which, remember, include all the conditions we chose for this life including family, beliefs, behavior, culture etc. and a "reality" is created with which we engage: the story. An image of this is then thrown onto the photographic plate and meets the original intention as an interference pattern.

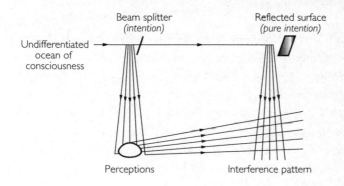

The Story = Intention + Created Reality

Hear me when I say nothing is solid. Reality is simply light waves transformed into particles by our intention and organized into patterns like the shapes created on the walls of a darkened cave by the flames of a flickering fire.

We spend so much time engrossed in the patterns that we fail to appreciate that the power is in the intention and not in the result. If our intention can create such diverse shapes it also has the power to dissolve these and create something different in the *blink of an eyelid.* All that holds something in form is our knowing that it exists where such inner knowing or intuition is one of the most powerful creative forces available to us at the time. When we only believe, hope or wish that it's true, the lack of conviction causes our intention to be weak and hence we find it difficult to both create well or to dissolve.

Now if the original intention and the created reality are congruent, and when our observer beam of coherent light, our wisdom, shines upon the interference pattern, a holographic image is produced and we see everything clearly with an expansion in consciousness.

We know ourselves through our creations and our consciousness grows.

However, such insight may not appear directly but only by making subtle changes which may take place over days or lifetimes! For instance, *I want to enhance self-worth (original intention)* and *receive an offer for a job where the salary is lower than I believe I deserve (reality)*. Due to the distortions that occur as the intention passes through my perceptions, the connection between thought and reality is not clear, and I'm left in the middle of a confusing interference pattern. But I have choices:

1. I can refuse the job, complaining about their stingy attitude and that they don't know quality when they see it, and continue the perception that is based on feelings of unworthiness and resentment. *This maintains the interference pattern as a mass of confusion and consciousness remains stagnant.*

2. I can shine a little light (the second light of wisdom on the subject) and say, *"Could this have anything to do with me?"* *The ghost of a holographic pattern starts to appear although stage 3. is required to bring the hologram fully alive.*

3. You consciously choose to change your approach at the next job interview and develop a firmer sense of self-worth with the ability to state clearly your requirements and be willing to make non-emotional decisions based on their response. *This approach creates a congruency between my intention and the result* and the hologram

comes alive and my consciousness increases not only because of receiving the salary I requested but because my intention was fulfilled through enhancement of my self-esteem.

It's not always easy to see what needs to change when you're in the middle of pain and disappointment. Some questions that shed a light on the subject include:

* *What have I learnt or gained from this experience?*

* *What changed because of this experience?*

* *What emotions were aroused because of the situation? Emotions, especially if they are exaggerated or inappropriate (laughing when we should cry), provide us with signposts as to why we drew this event towards us.*

* *Knowing that we are not here to suffer or be punished, what wisdom would you like to take from the experience?*

Often due to previous experience we have a certain *angle* or opinion on the situation which may prevent us from having an unbiased point of view. As the angle we perceive the holographic plate is so important to the degree of clarity, it's often useful to engage the services of a friend or therapist who approaches the situation with a different viewpoint or angle and is willing to provide the second laser light by shining their own *steady coherent light onto our problems or confusion.* You may also have the experience of someone offering a reflection of your situation that provides the *same mirror image* and suddenly you can see it all clearly.

Other ways to bring the holograph alive and hence achieve greater self-realization are by:

1. Meeting our own *mirrors* in the world. I always remind myself that when I see three people in a row with the same problem and give them wonderful advice then perhaps it's me who needs to listen. There are no

coincidences and such clients provide us with a wonderful reflection of ourselves until the hologram is revealed

2. Increasing consciousness over repeated expression of the same incident with subtle changes until we *get it, the light dawns* and we shout out loud, *"Ah-ha!"* as intention and perception of reality correspond and another petal of our soul is revealed

3. Honing the skills of the detached observer or our inner wisdom which provide the second laser light.

So, to summarize, we are constantly creating interference patterns between our intention and our creations and they become visible and conscious when we are willing to:

* change our angle of perception, releasing unhelpful beliefs and opening our minds to innocence and wisdom

* open our hearts through the clearing of disheartening emotions and reconnecting to the soul's resonance with compassion and joy

* center mind, body and spirit in the present, focusing attention and energy until a clear, coherent light is created.

One final insight is that when we enter this Earth, our *twin flame*, the flash of light that creates us, remains in a discarnate space, holding the intention for this incarnation. In other words, the twin flame is the reference beam while we are the direct beam. It is said that this is the reason why so many people seek a "soul mate" within the physical world, for somewhere they know the presence of their twin flame. It is however very rare that they should be on the planet at the same time, for their purpose is to hold the sacred space where magic can take place, knowing that a sacred marriage awaits them.

* * *

Healing through the hologram

There are an increasing numbers of therapeutic practices that work
with the principle of the hologram. For my own part, I believe
that our body, like this planet, is a library of knowledge and wisdom, storing thousands of years of experience and available to
us if we just have the right *key codes* to access the information.
I see the body as a mini holographic universe giving access to collective consciousness including the Akashic or wisdom records
of the individual.

The macrocosm expressed in the microcosm

I've come to appreciate that even though the cells of the body
are constantly renewing themselves, the energy underlying their
existence is the same. In a similar way, even though an individual has experienced an assortment of lifetimes, changing gender,
culture and shape frequently, the basic sacred geometry and hence
vibration of the human frame has remained the same.

I also see that because of the close relationship between the eyes
and pure light, the eyes are the one consistent part of the soul's
journey witnessing consciousness throughout time in a similar
manner that light holds the memory of anything that it has touched
throughout history. This is why I believe the study of the iris, *iri-
dology*, is so accurate in the exploration of mind, body and spirit
and why the eyes are truly the window of the soul, revealing its
journey within this Universe and beyond.

By simply looking with a soft gaze into the eyes of another person we are provided with a deeper understanding of their essence,
enhanced by the ancient tradition of touching foreheads which
allows us to access the inner or third eye. This energy center with
its two lobes, similar to the underlying pituitary gland, is believed
by the Ancient People to represent the tail of a great whale, with
the nose as the body of the whale. For many, the touching of

foreheads allows each person to "see" the other and especially their history, for the whale is the record keeper.

This is a powerful method of entering the hologram although in the main most of my clients would prefer a slightly more conventional approach. Hence, I usually have the client seated and start by setting up a sacred space, preferably with the client's assistance so that I enter their hologram with honor, compassion and without prejudging the result. In my belief nobody should enter the space of another, especially consciously, without receiving a **verbal** agreement, although it happens all the time, not always to the benefit of the recipient:

"You look tired today" they say, which strangely has never made me feel better!

Once the sacred space is formed, I then use my eyes or index finger as a laser beam to clarify my focus of vision and tap into the holographic universe as expressed through the particular perceptions of this individual, knowing that each of us will reveal a slightly different aspect of the whole. I commonly enter through *keyholes* which present themselves as pain or tension within the body, remembering that pain always means there is a part of the individual awaiting reconnection. Sometimes, however, I'm guided to enter through a calm and steady keyhole and progress slowly to the seat of the problem, advising me that this is an ancient issue often arising from previous lives.

In a similar way that a geologist would read the sediment of the Earth to understand its history, I literally read the memory stored in that area of body, layer by layer. I will also find myself following an energy line into the lives of ancestors, soul family, the planet and anywhere this light energy or consciousness has ever traveled. Sometimes to clarify an insight, I move my position to change my angle of view or expand my "visual field" to take in more of the environment.

I see the keyhole as an opening into multi-dimensional consciousness and, on many occasions, I describe what I see and

allow the client to travel with me so that the process becomes a shamanistic experience. On other occasions, the client actually journeys through their own body with me as the passenger which deepens the impact of the experience. As with the body talk, the healing comes not from an intellectual awareness but from the sharing of symbols which, entering a deeper area of the left brain, awakens a memory and activates the healing process. These symbols may include words, feelings, colors, pictures, smells and phrases, they stimulate the part of us that knows wholeness, releasing any blocks or knots in the energy line, leading to healing and the raising of vibration of that particular thread of consciousness.

Here is a journey into the human hologram:

Patty came to see me with chronic problems as a result of a broken clavicle some three years previously which was still giving her pain. Moving through the keyhole, I asked what had been happening in her life at the time of the accident. At first she said, "Nothing," and then, after a few moments, told me she had been having an affair which she was not proud about and that ended soon after the accident. I then started to see cowboy boots that didn't seem to belong to her. Amazed she told me she was fascinated with such boots, owning several pairs. Then I saw her strapped down to a railway line by her feet and hands.

"What are you doing there?" I asked, and without a pause she replied, *"I was a whore and was being killed for stealing from...a*

man in cowboy boots," we chimed in unison. And guess what part of her body was hit first by the train? Her clavicles.

For lifetimes her body had held this memory of shame and punishment that had reared its head again during the affair where there was a chance she would "steal" someone else's husband. Her body obviously decided to step in and remind her of the consequences which hopefully saved her greater pain in the long run. We spent time looking at her tendency to take what did not belong to her in order to feel superior even though she was really attempting to hide her shame. Through healing and forgiveness there was a dramatic improvement in the condition of the clavicle although I believe it will always have a little distortion in its shape as a loving reminder.

* * *

Past-life memories

When we work with the hologram and webs of energy it's not important to believe in past lives because we are simply examining a story or sequence of events that have been woven around an intention so that we may increase consciousness. Just as we know that spirit guides will change their form from, for instance, Native American to Chinese sage, depending who they are speaking to, so different life dramas are presented to us so that we might know ourselves more fully.

When I work with the hologram, I'm often faced with several scenarios with different outcomes but often involving the same players around a common theme. Sarah's issue was *truth.*

Sarah *presented with nodules on her vocal cords which were causing her problems as she worked as a teacher. She was a small woman who appeared shy and rather unassuming and yet, on deeper inspection, I saw a passion and fire that burnt within and* *it was obvious that Sarah was no pushover.*

As I entered the hologram through the throat which was the key-hole, I was bombarded with a range of images all related to this area and in particular to the issue of speaking her truth and on some occasions, its opposite. These included:

* The man in the 1800s who was pompous and dictatorial and liked the sound of his own voice, believing that his truth was all that mattered.

* The woman in the 1600s who was hung as a witch for speaking the truth even though her skill as a midwife had saved many lives.

* The child in 1500 BC who had prior knowledge of the imminent ambush by the enemy but who was ignored as he was seen as a simpleton.

* The woman whose tongue was cut out for lying.

* The monk who lived by a simple truth which allowed him to lead a Godly life.

* The lawyer who struggled daily to defend his clients despite their lies which eventually led him to drink.

And in this life, Sarah was subjected to four years of sexual abuse by a well-respected priest and then almost disowned when she attempted to tell the truth, followed by an early marriage to a man who lied about his frequent liaisons outside the marriage.

The year the nodules appeared was difficult for Sarah as she had observed certain senior figures at the school misappropriate funds and she was at odds whether to speak up or stay quiet. Fortunately, the illness helped her with the decision and she was given early retirement on the grounds of ill-health. However, we worked together for several months finding a way she could use her voice without fear and finding peace for all the parts of the self that had helped her to learn about the energy line of truth.

Global consciousness

In the past few years we have seen increasing numbers of people making the choice to live more congruent lives and honor their spiritual core values. These individuals *walk their talk* and are found in every arena of society often recognizable by their desire to create a common unity and unconcerned by their own personal needs.

As this global consciousness expands, the coherent light it produces shines upon interference patterns that have as yet been "unseen" and we hear in the news that certain "discoveries" have been made. What has happened is that these "objects" have been held in other levels of awareness such as the fourth dimensional world of dreams, until our consciousness reached a sufficient level to make them real. The ancient people such as the Incas knew how to raise the frequency of objects so that they were no longer present in the 3D world and to hide them in the fourth dimension, far away from the invaders of their country. Hence the unprofitable search by the early Spaniards for the golden city of El Dorado which had been neatly lifted into another dimension. Fortunately, the prophets of these cultures see these dark times as over and, with the consciousness of humanity expanding, it's now time for these objects to be returned to assist the planet in its transition.

There is also an increasing number of people whose psychic skills allow them to see, hear, smell or touch these other worlds. The next step is to be able to move freely between the dimensions accompanied by our body, which is true *ascension*. At this level we meet the shape shifters who are adept at changing form to become whatever is required in the moment and exist alongside us on this planet. One aspect of this is the phenomenon of transfiguration, which I have observed many times. Here you may be sitting across from another person when their face starts to transform, revealing layers of personalities that the soul has worn from time to time, some pleasant and some decidedly unsavory.

I have come to understand that I am merely an observer and not to take it personally, as the individual is often unaware of what is happening. However, it gives me a clearer picture of the many characters present within the room and which one may be running the show!

An important comment to make concerning holograms is that just as our personal intention can create a reality involving life, imagine the effect of mass thought on the manifestation of a reality. (I'm not using the word consciousness as much of this is unconscious.) You see it happening around sports teams, spiritual leaders and political leaders, where large crowds focus on a result and the Universe, as it is programmed to do, meets the thought with the same energy (the law of karma). If these masses only want love for that person or group, then they receive love, and if they bring hate, that is what is achieved. However, in many cases the intention is not pure but tainted with conditions, and hence when the group sends love, their message has expectations attached.

The result is that if the person on whom this energy is being bestowed has not developed a strong self-worth and a detachment from approval or criticism, they become *taken over* by the desires of the masses and the resultant universal energy and lose their own sense of identity to this holographic image that has overwhelmed them.

I offer this as a wake-up call to all of us to understand the power of the mind, especially when there is little true responsibility for the creation of thoughts. I believe the future will revolve around virtual reality technology. But please remember we are already living in a virtual reality field and the only way in which you are going to know whether it resonates with your truth is to test it through your intuition, feeling into the vibration of your heart and hearing the wisdom of your mind.

* * *

A final story reminds me that how I live my life is literally in my hands. Some years ago, I'd been working long hours in practice and finding myself more and more overwhelmed by the pain and suffering of the clients. I was walking down a road, telling a friend how I felt when I received a clear image of the solution. *I saw myself holding a section of the web of consciousness in my hand and knew that this represented my present work life with all its demands. With that I let go and it sprang back into the matrix of the web above. Surprised, I said; "It can't be that easy?"*

"Oh, but it always has been," came the reply. "It's only you who insists on holding on so tightly. Now, what would you like to create in your life?"

At that point, I came to appreciate the ease by which I could release what I thought was for life and understood that reality was about having the courage to let go and trust.

Chapter Five

Sacred Geometry and Sacred Sites

The human form as a sacred site and its relationship to phi

As we emerged onto this planet we, like many other of its inhabitants, mimicked the role of the sacred sites by becoming transformers and containers of energy between the webs. Mankind's unique position came from:

1. Our physical design, including the complex network of energy that flows through us and our carbon-based structure which, like crystals, has the capacity to store information within its lattice.

2. The ability to be self-conscious with its facet of free will.

Together they allow us to draw an idea down from above, pass it through our body and manifest the idea into form. Then, as we release our attachment to the form, we take the energy from the experience as wisdom back up through our body and offer this new consciousness to the web above. Thus our role is to be a transformer of light energy from wave to form and then back to wave again and hence achieve the status of alchemist of spirit.

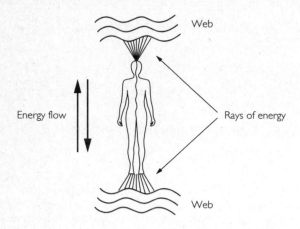

When we look at ourselves in a mirror and then compare ourselves with a supermodel, we appreciate there are subtle differences; OK, not so subtle! I look at my muscular legs and realize that they were never meant for the cat-walk but rather to run up and down the hills and glens of Scotland. So I am out of proportion? No, according to sacred geometry, we are all in "perfect shape" for the task of being a creative transformer of energy.

Phi (Ø) is a ratio that has been known from ancient times and was found to express the frequency of perfect creative activity. It is present in the dimensions of culturally important structures such as the Parthenon in Athens and the Great Pyramid in Egypt. The ratio of phi is:

$\frac{1}{2}$ + square root of 5 divided by 2 = 1.6180339
(commonly taken to 3 decimal points at 1.618)

Leonardo da Vinci understood the importance of this ratio as depicted in many of his famous diagrams, as did the Greeks who fully appreciated that beauty is seen when this ratio is expressed in art and hence the production of exquisite statues which, still today, cause you to stop and wonder.

Our body as a transformer of creative energy was designed specifically for this function. Here are a few of it's dimensions that correspond to the phi ratio i.e. when one measurement is 1.618 greater than the other. Perhaps you would like to follow along with a measuring rule or tape!

* The *navel* is seen by Buddhists as an obvious site to consider the center of the Universe, and in the newborn baby it indeed occupies that position. But as we grow, it moves to take up a new position as a phi ratio, with the distance from feet to navel being 1.618 greater than the distance from navel to head. Apparently the male's phi ends slightly above the navel and the female's phi is slightly below, allowing for curves!

* The length of each bone in the fingers and toes has a phi ratio to the next bone

* The length of the hand is in phi ratio to the length of the lower arm

* The length of the foot is in phi ratio to the lower leg bone

* The length of lower arm bone is in phi ratio to the upper arm bone

* The length of the lower leg bone is in phi ratio to the upper leg bone, etc.

And these are exact ratios, no mistake … so tell that to the next person who says you've got odd-looking arms and legs!

Given our divine purpose, it is essential that we honor this by:

1. Clearing the energy lines that pass through our being of any blockages or knots that may have occurred lifetimes ago or may indeed be connected to ancestors or soul family. This includes working with the chakras and the meridians.

2. Reversing the polarity of the lines that may be obstructing the flow of energy and reminds us to honor duality in order to achieve unity.

3. Engaging fully with this Earth while maintaining a healthy link to the web above.

4. Taking responsibility for the development of self-consciousness which involves retrieving energy or power that was lost, focusing attention to the place of presence and opening the mind and heart to all the possibilities available.

✳ ✳ ✳

The more we engage with the energies coming through our head and our feet, the more we realize that they are not separate but a continuum in the shape of the *torus* with us positioned in the center.

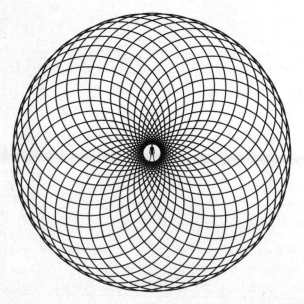

Torus

The torus is known to be a self-perpetuating form which, in this world, is a rare commodity, and teaches us that when we are willing to step into the center of our world the energy flow through us and around us is eternal. This same pattern is found in two other important structures: the first being the heart where it has been shown that the organ sits in the center of an energetic torus which extends at least 12–15 feet from the body; the second is the sun which sits at the center of a toroidal solar system maintaining the flow of energy on a much larger scale.

Imagine torus within torus all centered on the nucleus of the smallest unit of our being, each self-perpetuating and feeding the other, and then you understand the nature of the Christ Consciousness Grid.

In geometric terms the sequence that leads to the formation of the torus can be seen as follows:

1. First we seek to complete one cycle of creativity:

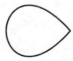

2. We then express its duality and create the sign of *infinity:*

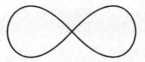

3. As we extend our awareness further and further out to the extremes and move between the poles of awareness, we start to experience the flow of energy around a central point:

4. In time, the dual poles of existence draw together in order to know unity and an important symbol called the *vesica piscis* is produced where the circumference of one circle passes through the center of another. This formation creates access to light consciousness in its purest form and is created in name of love and unification.

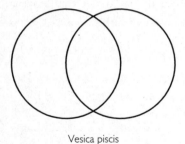

Vesica piscis

Eventually, when the multiple dualities each create a vesica piscis then we see the formation of the torus with its seven spiraling sections which together take us to a new octave of heightened awareness.

The golden mean and Fibonacci's numbers

The phi ratio is related to the formation of the *Golden Rectangle* which is the starting point for the creation of spirals and is formed by one side of a rectangle being 1.618 greater than the other.

If we then continue to divide the rectangle, we see the emergence of the Golden Mean Spiral which forms the basis for the

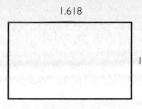

1.618

Ratio 1:1.618

Golden Rectangle

layout of many important sacred sites, including the positioning of the Egyptian pyramids, around the Great Pyramid. This reveals that ancient civilizations knew the importance to their own survival of recreating these creative spirals, maintaining both their connection to the Source and the flow of energy through their own body. The Golden Mean is also found throughout our world in the movement of the galaxy and the shapes of the nautilus shell, sunflower, pine cone and many other wonderful formations. Their existence in Nature is a constant reminder of our Divine purpose stimulating the alchemist within.

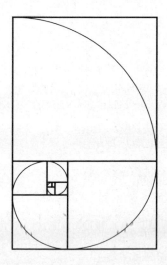

Golden Mean Spiral

It's perhaps interesting to note that the pine cone energetically stimulates the *pineal gland* because of a similarity in shape (and of course in name) and that pine essence is commonly used by those who wish to enhance their creative union between spirit and matter. Personally, I have always found great solace and inspiration while walking amongst pine trees whether in the highlands of Scotland or here in southern California.

Finally, in our study of phi, we move to the ground breaking work of the mathematician Leonardo Fibonacci, who showed that phi can be reached when we add successive numbers to each other starting with the number 1. Although the initial additions do not follow phi, the later ones certainly do, and the ratio continues as far as you wish to take it.

Additions:

| $1 + 1 = 2$ | $2 + 1 = 3$ | $3 + 2 = 5$ | $5 + 3 = 8$ | $8 + 5 = 13$ |

Ratio:

| 1.0 | 2.0 | 1.5 | 1.666 | 1.600 |

Additions:

| $13 + 8 = 21$ | $21 + 13 = 34$ | $34 + 21 = 55$ | $55 + 34 = 89$ | $89 + 55 = 144$ |

Ratio:

| 1.625 | 1.619 | 1.618 | 1.618 | 1.618 |

It is interesting to note that if the management structure of any corporation is built on the principles of Fibonacci's numbers then success and creative abundance is almost guaranteed.

1

1

2

3

5

8

* * *

SACRED SITES

Sites such as Newgrange remind us of our sacred duty and our ability to achieve the sacred marriage both within ourselves and between us and the Source. Other important locations include Stonehenge and Avebury in England, Jerusalem, Cusco and Machu Picchu in Peru, Palenque in Mexico, Uluru in Australia, Lhasa in Tibet, the Ganges in India, Chartres in France, Mount Shasta in northern California and the volcanoes of Haleakala and Mauna Loa in Hawaii, although there are thousands of other sites marked by temples, stone circles, medicine wheels, carvings and a mere sense of presence.

Increasing numbers of studies show that each site, connected as it is to the webs of energy, will produce very similar observations or symbols for those who choose to sit, meditate or dream within its vibrational field. These sites represent a place where the veil between the dimensions is extremely thin, hence allowing us to "travel" to previously unchartered parts of ourselves, a fact well known by the Ancient people. The symbols we receive pass into our left brain, bypassing a more superficial level of knowing and drawing to the surface a deeper intellect, allowing us to remember a potential that waits within.

The only words of caution I will sound are similar to those to a child in a candy store: it's important to have some idea what you seek when entering such locations and not be persuaded to buy or eat something that later you will regret. Sacred sites have been used for all manner of rituals over the ages, some affirming and some definitely dark. Choose your site using a wise heart, allow your intention to be clear and *please* be careful **not** to carry more fear into the place in your desire to "cleanse" its energy. Despite man's lack of finesse and poor appreciation of these places, the spiritual central of the site is not damaged, It's only covered by a fine film of human *astral and lower mental waste* which can easily be passed through when your intention is one of respect and compassion.

Sound and sacred sites

Further research on sacred sites is emerging from Paul Devereux, a veteran worker in the field who, in his book, *Stone Age Soundtracks*, looks at studies carried out by a team known as the International Consciousness Research Laboratories (ICRL). They traveled the world testing sound waves that were found within sites as diverse as *kivas* in New Mexico and Newgrange in Ireland. They found that despite the variety in shape, size and construction, all sites yield a frequency between 95–120 Hz and commonly within the band of 110–112, which is the range of a male voice.

The team proffered the hypothesis that suggested that the sites were the location of rituals involving male voices with the structure providing a resonating vessel, enhancing the reverberation and creating the illusion of the presence of a great god. However, it is also possible that when we harmonize with the frequency of 110 Hz we find our consciousness taken to new levels of awareness with the construction designed to enhance our tones.

Sound has been associated with many of these sites whether made by the wind blowing through the stones or produced by shamans as part of a ceremony. I have been present in many sites where alcoves were created in the walls of the building specifically for the purpose of toning, even though the official line was that they were used for decoration and flower displays! When I toned into these recesses, usually using the *oo* sound, I have found that when I sound the right frequency and pitch, my voice started to produce overtones and I knew I had entered a vast multi-dimensional arena.

Jonathan Goldman, a leader in sound therapy and with a four-octave voice, tells a story in his book, *Healing Sounds*, about a visit to Palenque in Mexico where he descended into a darkened area at the base of the temple. Here in the darkness he began to tone harmonics and, as he did, the room became illuminated. His own research led him to reach the following conclusion:

Through the use of vocally created harmonics it is possible to stimulate the pineal gland to produce light which radiates out through the subtle bodies.

The pineal gland is rich in the hormone melatonin, a photo transducer with the capacity to absorb and convert sound energy into light. This appears to occur through the hormone triggering the release of a substance that contains phosphorus, which is known to produce light. Melatonin is also present in the heart which is interesting as we often relate this area to the note or resonance of the soul. Is this what is meant by *glowing with joy?*

Energy lines across time

As we traverse the globe, it is possible to tap into many sites that are sacred to the underlying webs or grid systems and may find ourselves being transported back in time to a previous association, with echoes in our present-day life. This happened to me during a trip to Rhodes, the beautiful and historic Greek island. As I was walking up an ancient cobbled street, my foot stepped on a particular stone transporting me back in time to the early 12th century when the Knight's Templars traveled through Rhodes on their way to the Holy Land. These keepers of eternal wisdom dated back to early Egypt and were contracted to protect the grid of Christ Consciousness at all costs although eventually they became corrupted by their own power.

As I continued to walk, I could feel my body take on a new posture to accommodate the weight of the heavy cloak, with its distinctive cross, now hanging across my shoulders and stretching down to the floor. As this Knight, I strode up the cobbles, troubled by my own thoughts and oblivious to any 20th-century sightseers, I inwardly asked, *"What troubles you?"* To which my 12th-century self said, *"We were meant to protect the Christ Line but everything is going wrong; it's bad."*

"What can I do to help?" I enquired, almost afraid of disturbing him while he was deep in thought. But he heard me and replied, *"Feed my children"* and before I could ask what he meant, my connection was lost as I quickly side-stepped a large group of camera-snapping tourists.

* * *

A postscript to the story is that when I was 11, I decided not to join the Girl Guides but opted for a training as a St John's Ambulance volunteer, offering my first-aid services to events around the country. For seven years I wore the distinct uniform which included in its design a large cross, only to learn later that this modern-day organization evolved from the hospitals run by the Knight's Templars.

There are no coincidences on this Earth!

Power lines and the underworld

Since then I have become increasingly fascinated by the lines of energy that, as part of the web, criss-cross our planet and that I now realize are far more valuable than any gold or silver mine or oil reserves. Some, like the Christ Grid found primarily in Egypt and South and Central America, or the Michael/Mary line which twists and turns through southern England, have been relegated to the arena of mythology, ending up in stories concerning dragons, serpents and pagan rites. And yet those who seek power are, even today, obsessed with gaining control of these lines, especially their entry points or portals, for it is believed that whoever controls these controls the world.

At the end of the war, amongst the rubble of Berlin, were found a group of Tibetan monks who had together committed suicide. There was much puzzlement as to why these monks were so far from home and why they had died. This led to some intriguing detective work that unearthed Hitler's interest in the world within our world and his allocation of vast sums of money and troops to find these portals, one of which exists in Lhasa and hence the Tibetan connection. I have been taken to visit this "underworld" in my meditations and have experienced the green lights and the perfectly still air which are present in the tunnels that lead down to this inner world.

The story goes that at times in our history when the Earth experienced cataclysmic changes, such as at the end of Atlantis and Lemuria, people naturally had three places to go: into the sea, up into the mountains and down into the earth. It is believed that even after the planet became habitable again, many chose to stay in their new homes as their bodies had adapted to the relevant environment.

Hence there are stories of those who live within the waters, such as in the crystal city beneath Lake Titicaca, and that when Atlantis was engulfed by the seas, some of the inhabitants shape-shifted into dolphins and carried the gift of intuition to Delphi in Greece, the seat of the great oracle. (Delphi is Greek for Dolphin.) There are also tales of those who live amongst some of the tallest mountains of the world enshrined within stories about Shangrila and Shamballa.

Then there are also reports of groups who live within the Earth and of outsiders searching for the portals into these worlds, never being seen again or returning as young as the day they disappeared even though 70 years may have elapsed. The entry points to this inner world are known to exist throughout the world, and they exhibit similar characteristics. These include a stillness unbroken by any bird song or animal call, a foul smell which many believe to be some type of dangerous gas, discouraging any unwanted visitors, and a vivid fluorescent green light which appears to be connected to the ability to reproduce photosynthesis so the inhabitants can remain underground.

I and several others believe we have established contact during meditation or visual imagery work with the beings who inhabit this world. The common consensus is that they are ambivalent about forming a relationship with those of the middle world as they feel we have little to offer and believe that we would only misuse any gifts they gave us until we started to *live in the real world*. Access to these other realms is easier in countries such as Ireland, New Zealand and South America where respect for the earth and its "little people" is still present in the culture. Elsewhere, I have come across a thick layer of granite, of unknown origin, separating the two worlds and obviously causing difficulties for those who wish to develop dialogue. I believe our task is to find a way through this dense structure but this can only happen when we seek union and not power.

It's interesting to note that officially we have been discouraged from journeying into the *underworld*, often synonymous with *hell*. Even though I appreciate there are different interpretations for such a term, I'm starting to suspect that anything we were taught to fear probably hides a rich source of information and natural power.

There is one other place where spirits exist who, at one time, walked this Earth and that is amongst the Nature Kingdoms. There are many stories of Elfin beings living amongst trees and plants, Dwarfs who exist within the stone kingdoms and Nymphs who swim within the seas. These stories of mystical beings who live in the twilight zone between man and Nature are not myths. There are even those who have chosen this time to live a mortal life although, when you look at their physique, you get the sense that they could quite easily merge back into the frequency of water, trees or stones and never be seen again.

These spirits are closely related to the Age of Lemuria when heaven and earth were still energetically related and they maintained the flow of spiritual force between the two. As we as humans became more self-conscious and obsessed with technology, we lost interest in these entities, believing that we could survive without their help and abusing the planet to meet our own needs. Yet, here we are in the 21st century with Nature rebelling against our lack of co-operation and indicating that perhaps this is the time for a little humility and respect if we are going to prevent further droughts, floods, wild fires and starvation.

There is a story about the Mayans, a highly sophisticated culture who understood the close relationship between man and Nature. Their golden age was long before the coming of the Spaniards to Central America, the latter meeting the remnants of a civilization similar to Egyptians in Cairo today who would have difficulty explaining the building of the Great Pyramid. It is said that the culture developed on the Hawaiian Island of Moloka'i better known in the last century for its leper colony. When they outgrew the island, they moved to Central America where they expanded and became highly successful and accomplished. However, it is said that they never lost their collective soul, and one day they realized that their path was leading them further and further from their spiritual truth and with one accord decided to return to the world of spirit and become one with the trees and the plants. This certainly provides a plausible explanation for the sudden disappearance of a whole culture which has been the source of mystery for centuries.

The word Maya means *illusion* and defines a group who were master magicians and who probably designed the holographic realities that are fundamental to our life today. Indeed their knowledge of the illusion of time and space allowed them to travel with ease across the dimensions, setting into place "time locks" which could only be opened when humanity reached certain levels of consciousness.

Opening these locks provides us with access into different paradigms of awareness and can only be found if you seek with the heart of love and the mind of a child. I have been privileged to experience these doorways and enter into the dimensions beyond, having received permission from the *door keeper* who seeks certain conditions as outlined below. On many occasions,

I had to close my mind to the information being given by the official guide who, with the best will in world, was merely repeating relatively modern archaeological conclusions.

There are simple Universal guidelines that express the ritual and etiquette required to create a *right relationship* with any beings of spirit whether human, of the ether or belonging to the elementals or Nature Kingdoms. It is strange to me that so much ritual and procedure is applied to talking with God and yet is absent when spending time with other people, animals etc., all of whom radiate the Divine spark.

The future of our world is concerned with the willingness to stretch out a hand and create relationships based on respect, honor and the appreciation that we meet our God everywhere within this Universe. Hence the phrases found in ancient cultures such as *Namaste* and *Wiracocha* which translate as:

> *"May the god within me meet the god within you."*

It is perhaps only within the human race that such lines of etiquette have lost their relevance, mainly due to fear and self-absorption, especially in individuals who are deluded into believing that they and their little lives are so important that respect for others can be abandoned.

We are already witnessing the results of man playing god and the lack of respect for the spirit world through the dramatic changes in weather systems and this is only the beginning.

It is hard for those within the so-called progressive, modern world to appreciate that the basis for creativity and abundance comes from the formation of sacred space. This requires the establishment of a rhythm which sets the tone of the relationship or meeting. It ensures that everybody is coming from the same starting point and is the reason why old cultures continue the ritual of offering nourishment or small-talk at the commencement of any discussion. Indeed it is considered the sign of an immature soul to fail to set the rhythm before getting down to business and predicts a poor long-term outcome.

These same lines of etiquette are required of us when we chose to interact with any of those within the subtle realms, remembering that at sacred sites there is always a guardian or door keeper whose permission we need to seek first. The guidelines outlined below are the rules that define a true alchemist, without which his/her practices flounder on the rocks of inexperience and lack of commitment to the task.

1. *Setting the rhythm of the relationship*

    a) The Native Americans talk of beginning any meeting through the door of the South: the door of innocence and of the child. The world of spirit is not interested in your grandiose ideas, in the university degrees that plaster your walls or how much money you earn. It is **not** asking you to save or heal it for it's still connected to the Source where eternal health is possible.

    I was told this story by an Inca Shaman who recalls a friend's attempt to enter the 4th dimension after much practice and deep study. He finally achieved his goal and was met at the gate by the guardian who congratulated him on his success and offered him a glistening golden key. The friend's eyes widened at the sight of the gift and his ego glowed as he reached out to take the key. Immediately, he found himself back in the 3rd dimension having failed the test of detachment.

    Can you approach in humility (not humbleness and grovelling), with wonder and curiosity and with gratitude based on respect and honor? And most of all can you put aside your seriousness and enter with laughter and joy?

    b) Now since small-talk or the partaking of drinks may not be appropriate, the scene is set through the arts which not only set the rhythm but entertain the spirit and reveal your particular frequency or vibration. This may involve song, humming or toning or we may choose to dance or move to inner music. For our own part, through the arts, we open our minds to right-brain awareness, intuitive knowing and hence a connection to other realms; we move into the spirals of *cyclical awareness*.

It is our responsibility to attract the attention of the spirit world, for they are ambivalent about forming an alliance with us due to our lack of co-operation in the past.

We need them more than they need us, for without this reconnection we are a dying race.

2. *Using the power of wisdom to communicate and state our needs*

The ability to speak with clarity and without emotion is a gift and is the surest way of manifesting our needs. When our words are laden with emotions, the spirit world hears us as if we are speaking from within the deepest ocean. In truth, they already know our questions and wishes, for to them it is a telepathic universe without secrets, but it is important that we hear our own words. So often we speak with *forked tongue* saying one thing while meaning another, often due to a fear of rejection. And because of the confusion the very thing we fear happens, and we leave unheard and rejected. It is only when we stand in our power and speak from our heart that we are heard. In the medicine wheel this stage is represented by the door of the North, the place of *wisdom* and the mature adult.

3. *The willingness to become what we seek*

This phase is one that many novice alchemists fail to understand and hence achieve, for it asks that we should merge with the subject of our request or conversation. Why would we expect anything or anybody to work with us, if we are not willing to know their spiritual essence fully? This is the true meaning of unconditional love: *to know and meet another without conditions or agenda which includes releasing any concept of pity, superiority or even inferiority.* Imagine every meeting, especially within the corporate world, including this component where you could not request someone to act for you unless you had first-hand experience from their perspective, relevant to present-day circumstances.

We are all one family in the consciousness of light whether we are talking with angels, masters, elves or a mosquito. To enter the web of Christ Consciousness asks us to dismantle the hierarchical systems which belong only to the limited three-D world

This is also the stage that requires a stable base and firm roots without which we can lose ourselves in these other realms leading to illnesses such as bipolar disorder (manic depression) and schizophrenia. I have met many who express this "oneness" as a blissful experience but then have great trouble in reconnecting to this reality.

So before we attempt to merge with the world of spirit, we first need to develop roots, either physically through feeling the ground through the soles of our feet, or through visual imagery where we see ourselves as a great mountain or tall tree with deep roots, anchoring us into the earth. Then, having successfully secured our stance, we create a sacred space through the vesica piscis, using the meditation given in the next chapter. This symbol of unity through love asks that we come from our hearts and not our heads, merging with the essence of the subject in question without becoming lost in it: *collective awareness.*

Hence we become the droplet of water, the wind that flows, the rays of the sun or the food that we seek to eat.

We *become* the source of our own answers which
emerge from the collective consciousness of the soul.

Once we have united with the frequency of our desire,
the spirit world sees that we can be trusted and can then
choose to work with us. In the medicine wheel, this is
the door of East: the door of Spirit.

4. *Returning to physical reality*

Now we are at the door of the West, the door of the
physical world where true magic occurs. Here we draw
the essence of spirit we met in the East into the world of
matter, anchoring the idea or desire into reality through
manifestation. This whole process has little meaning if
we cannot bring the knowledge or information back into
our world and transform it into action through the
alchemical process.

* * *

The path of the true alchemist is not for personal wealth, health
or favor but always seeks to benefit the greater good **without** interfering with the path of others. We are here to act in a way that
benefits all because of our interconnected nature without attachment to a result or through seeking self-gratification. It is the ability to connect on a deep and meaningful level with every aspect
of spirit, which fills our coffers with joy and satisfaction, and after
that little else is required, for everything else is illusion.
This is the paradox:

> *We have to make our intentions into matter*
> *to realize they don't matter.*

Chapter Six

Healing the Divide

Portals to these various realms are available to us all but as the ancient council book of the Mayans, *Popul Vuh*, states: *"The Truth is hidden from the searcher and the seeker,"* implying that the truth is only accessed by those who have soft eyes to see, hearts to feel, and who seek without hope for gain. They are often associated with rifts in the Earth's core, mirrored by a similar tear in the ether above, allowing easy access to the multi-dimensional levels of existence.

You only have to observe where wars have been continually fought over centuries to locate these portals, even though it has been fashionable to blame everything on religion. Yes, it's true that gods have often been the cause of the problem but usually little gods or siblings fighting each other for control of power, and that continues to this day. Look at Iraq (once Persia), South Africa, Kashmir, Afghanistan, Israel, Turkey, Tibet, Central America and many other areas where there are hot springs or frequent earthquake or volcano activity, including New York and California. These are the areas of power in the world and this has been known for thousands of years.

So instead of seeing these portals or rifts as places to embrace the various dimensions through the union of opposites, there has been a tendency to fight over such power and hence maintain separation and stagnation of growth and evolution for all. As a race, we have to decide collectively whether we choose to unite these forces, acknowledging and accepting both sides of the divide equally, or whether to remain at our present level of consciousness where our survival cannot be guaranteed.

In other words love and unity are NOT options:
they are a necessity.

An ancient method of drawing the two sides together is through the creation of the symbol called the *vesica piscis*. This sacred geometric shape is formed when the circumference of one circle passes through the center of another, creating a fish-shaped doorway in its center.

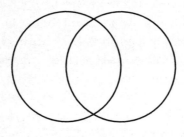

Vesica piscis

This oval shape is the entry point into inter-dimensional awareness, unity, ecstasy and Christ Consciousness which extends far beyond 2,000 years of history and evokes the soul's connection with its Source. In ancient tradition, it is said that a wound created in the trunk of a cedar tree, shaped in the form of the vesica piscis, allowed those who were ready to enter to access the library of collective consciousness.

However, as the story implies it's often only when we are willing to feel our wounds or sense of disconnection that we eventually come to a place of love and acceptance and, on entering the vesica piscis, allow healing to occur. We cannot enter the vesica piscis laden with expectations, bargaining rites and demands which merely serve as a defence against the fear of losing control. It's only by the willingness to be vulnerable while respecting and having compassion for everybody's wounds and fears that we can ever hope to find a platform for negotiations and hence end long-standing enmity. These rift areas around the world are calling us to meet and talk rather than fight, for the message of the vesica piscis is:

"For when two or more are gathered...there I am in the midst of them."

(St Matthew ch 18 v20).

* * *

If we are going to help heal the wounds of our race, we first have to accept and heal the wounds we carry within our own being. Wherever you have fear, hatred or shame, there is division within you and a part of you that seeks reconnection. To help in our journey the vesica piscis is naturally found at key transition areas in our body, urging us to find union between different poles of existence. These include:

* *The vulva of a woman,* an obvious location for initiation as the baby leaves a place of intimate connection and transits onto its individualized path. Here we leave behind a *collective experience* and start to develop *self-consciousness.*

* *The gap in the diaphragm* through which the major blood vessels and esophagus pass from the chest to the

abdomen and vica versa. In esoteric terms, this relates to the passage from the lower three chakras related to our *personal needs* to the upper chakras connected to our *transpersonal self*. At this point we make the decision to take responsibility for our own personal power and are ready to grasp the head of our personal power, kundalini energy and thread it through the *eye of the needle*, the vesica piscis.

As the Bible says, *"It is easier for a camel to go through the eye of a needle, than for a rich man to enter into the kingdom of God."*
(St Matthew ch 19 v24).

This comment is not asking us to deny ourselves the gifts of the physical world but only to release our attachment to them and ascend beyond the field of fear and neediness which limits our passage towards becoming a spiritualized human being.

* ✳ *The vocal cords* representing the transition from living by *our little will* to the *will of the Creator*. Our voice is a powerful creative tool, unfortunately often used indiscriminately showering others with energy that has no connection to the heart or to the wisdom of the soul. As we move through this vesica piscis our voice and mind become vehicles of expression for our higher self which is eternally linked to the Divine.

These first three sites are all related to the breath in one way or other and reflect the powerful influence that respiration plays in the timing and force of the creative process.

* ✳ *The eyes* are now known not only to receive input but to initiate the creative process, especially when the gaze is soft, and hence the understanding by the Ancient People of the power of the evil eye. The eyes sit at the threshold of the transformation of light energy moving it through its

various frequencies to reveal infinite levels of
consciousness. The vesica piscis at this level represents
the transition from a world of structure to one of pure
light where our inner and outer worlds become a true
reflection of each other and allow us to know our soul
without distraction, attachment or bias.

* * *

Finally, there are vesica piscis found within sacred buildings,
especially temples and churches built with an understanding and
respect for sacred geometry. If a rectangle is formed around the
fish-shaped portal, then the ratio of the sides is found to be
exactly 1 to the square root of 3. This ratio is found in the nave
of many ancient churches, reflecting that such a building was
never meant to be a place for sermons and sitting but for singing
and toning in harmony with the frequency of the structure itself.
In other words, the churches were designed specifically for us
to reach a level of vibration where we could find perfect union
with the Source.

* * *

Meditation to create a vesica piscis

The best way to create this beautiful, sacred design is to work with
a friend or partner who sits facing you. It's also possible to work
with a part of yourself you would like to meet either because of
their increased vantage point of wisdom or because you are having trouble integrating them and would like to know them on a
deeper level. You can even meet a person or guide from the world
of spirit, asking them to join you if they are available! If you have
no live being before you, it's still useful to place a chair in front
so you can create the sacred space.

Sit comfortably, close your eyes and, with the help of the breath, allow the body to start to relax. As you sink deeper into the chair or wherever you are sitting, continue to release any tension in the body using the breath.

As the muscles ease, on the out-breath let go of thoughts of the past and then the thoughts of the future, bringing your mind gently to the present, relaxed and focused only on the breath. Now take your awareness inside, conscious of the movement of the chest and perhaps the heart beating but only as a passing observation. And go deeper.

Move your awareness to the core of your being without effort or hurry and go deeper. From that place, take your awareness to the area of the heart chakra, the center of the chest and bring to mind a time when you have felt you heart open with feelings of joy, happiness and love. Perhaps it was with your grandchildren or with your partner or when watching a beautiful sunset or when your dog came to greet you. Whatever the experience, expand the feelings in the heart by adding color, sounds, aromas and touch and smile to yourself as the memory expands to include other people or a deepening of the connection.

Now imagine your heart is like a vessel or chalice, filling with joy and happiness from the experience. Watch and feel as it becomes full and the happiness starts to spread out first to your physical body (and especially to areas of disharmony or pain) and then to the subtle bodies. No effort, no forcing, just allowing as the love and joy radiates out from your heart. If the feeling starts to decrease, simply return to the memory and using visual, auditory or kinesthetic aids, fill the heart again.

Now the energy is radiating out beyond your body and in all directions around you, no effort. In particular, the joy spreads out towards your partner or towards the part of you with which you wish to engage. Simply allow the energy to flow without "sending" or trying, merging your joy with that of your partner or whoever sits opposite. Be conscious of their presence as your circles meet, observe the feeling without analysis. Let the joy continue to flow and allow yourself to bathe in the state of bliss, unity and peace that develops. If you can hold the memory with your eyes open, gently open your eyes and see how the flow may change when eye contact is added.

From this place, healing takes place naturally, although we can send out a specific intention on a wave of joy. It's also a wonderful place from which to communicate with someone where trust may have been an issue or when you wish to reach a deeper level of communion. If you are working with a part of yourself, you can ask this part questions and wait for answers directly into your heart without the need for words.

When you are complete, simply give silent thanks and slowly draw the energies back into your body and your heart, knowing that you have been enriched by the exchange and this place always awaits you.

* * *

Occasionally, I have also drawn spirit guides in to support the circles but this should be without effort and without the search for results. This exercise can be enriched further by adding toning using in particular, the *oo* and *ah* sounds which resonate with the sacral and heart chakras, both of which are relevant to this exercise of creating a sacred space of love, respect, nurturing and receptivity.

The vesica piscis is an ancient symbol used by millions over many eons and is dedicated to enabling mankind to reach a state of Christ Consciousness and hence to know unification and bliss. Enjoy.

The flower of life and the vesica piscis

When six people come together to create a much larger vesica piscis, they create a six-petalled flower with a central circle known as the *seed of life* which represents the beginning of life according to Divine Consciousness. The symbolism reflects the six days it took to create the world with the center circle as the day of rest or completion.

The Seed of Life

This can then be expanded to create the *flower of life* which consists of 19 interlacing circles surrounded by two concentric circles. Nineteen is important in numerology for it represents the beginning and the end, the alpha and the omega and this particular symbol is said to contain our cellular memory and is the matrix for all matter.

The Flower of Life

Finally, by removing the outer circles and adding another rotation, a design emerges called the *fruit of life* which consists of 13 completed circles. This represents the wisdom or fruit which is the result of living our reality and represents our ascension to the next level of awareness.

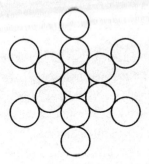

The Fruit of Life

Over the centuries, the magical qualities of the number 13 have been kept secret by cleverly calling it an *unlucky number* and referring to the unsuccessful mission of Jesus due to his 12th disciple, Judas. It is said that if he had not been included, then there would have only been 11 + 1 = 12, the number of cosmic order and salvation. And yet the mission was a Universal success, as Judas, a highly evolved soul, enabled the Christ energy to be revealed through the process of surrender, resurrection and then ascension. Thirteen is in fact connected to the spiraling nature of death and rebirth, each death allowing our inner light to shine more brightly.

It's interesting to note that in the last 2,000 patriarchal years, there has been a tendency to call anything that involves cycles or spirals as pagan and associate it with the undesirable qualities of feminine energy, including connection and sensitivity. Yet, these cycles ensure our existence, providing the nurturing light fuel for the soul and we cannot continue without honoring their importance. It is interesting to note that for the past 15 years, across the world, strange formations have appeared in the crops, 80 per cent within the UK, and often consisting of circles and spirals. Perhaps the

creators of these designs are attempting to awaken our inner serpent of creativity and encouraging us to spiral up towards our true
height and power.

* * *

These various symbols appearing out of the vesica piscis are seen
to represent the feminine face of creativity from birth through to
the harvest. By adding lines to the structure, male energy, we create the *Metatron's cube* which contains within it the five *Platonic
solids* from which all structures are built.

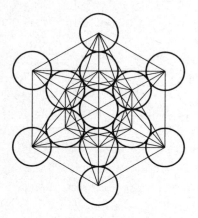

Metatron's Cube

To be a platonic solid, the configuration has to have all its faces
of the same size, its edges the same length and, if placed within
a sphere, all its points touching the edge. Those which conform
are as follows:

* ***The Tetrahedron*** (fire) made up of four equilateral
  triangles linked to creativity.

* ***The Cube or Hexahedron*** (earth) which has six faces
  associated with earthly order.

✳ **The Octahedron** (air) with eight faces of equilateral triangles associated with spiritual regeneration.

✳ **The Icosahedron** (water) with 20 faces of equilateral triangles symbolizing feminine wisdom or intuition.

✳ **The Dodecahedron** (ether) with 12 faces of pentagons or five-sided figures symbolizing divine order or will.

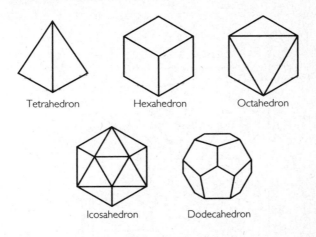

Tetrahedron   Hexahedron   Octahedron

Icosahedron   Dodecahedron

The Platonic Solids

When we look at Kabbalah, the Hebrew esoteric tradition, we see that its main symbol is the *Tree of Life*. This represents the 10 attributes of God, through which the lightning flash of Divine creative power moves in order that God can behold himself in the manifested form. The Tree is seen with its roots in heaven and its branches reaching down into the Earth and has within it the laws and principles which govern man and the universe. This important symbol, representing our very existence on the planet, can be superimposed onto the vesica piscis and then onto the seed, flower and fruit of life, unifying all facets of Creation, male and female.

Sacred geometry is the music by which our Universe was created and is the matrix in which we exist. Drawings of these symbols are found throughout the world and are understood to have played a major role in the spiritual teachings of all ancient cultures.

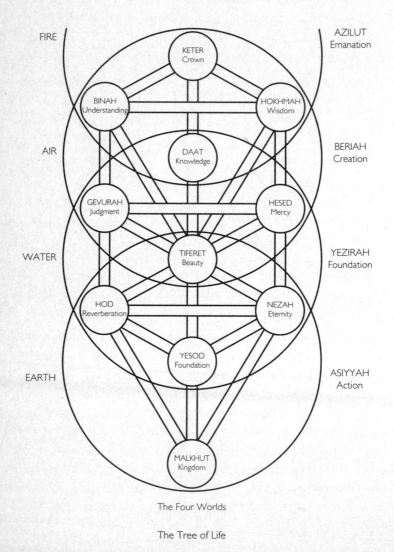

The Four Worlds

The Tree of Life

Chapter Seven

The Power of Intention

Since quantum physics has shown that intention is a major player in the creative process, let us explore its character further. The word comes from the Latin *tendere* which means to stretch or direct and can be likened to an archer pulling back his/her bow and, with all their strength, maintaining that stretch until they are ready to let the arrow fly towards its target. Such intention demands not only power but a focused and steady mind-heart already "seeing" the arrow find its mark.

Intention = Focus/Attention + Force/Power

As we set our intention, we create a frequency similar to a radio signal which has the capacity to crystallize light into form. By changing the intention, we can then dissolve that creation until it releases the light and we are once again left without form. For a successful conclusion we seek:

1. A powerful and coherent *force* which produces a strong signal. This is achieved by reassembling all the energies that have become lost, trapped or mutated into one integrated force.

2. Minimal scattering of *focus* or *attention* so that delivery
   of the message is accurate. This occurs through
   expansion of consciousness, which allows concentration
   from a place of discernment not limitation.

If we were to look at the symbolism of the bow and the arrow,
the arrow represents the masculine energies of force and clarity,
while the bow represents the feminine energies of focus and receptivity. However both aspects also contain a complementary component. Hence, the yin quality of the arrow is its willingness to
sacrifice itself for the cause, for the force or energy is usually extin-
guished in the name of success. The bow, on other hand, is like
the muscles of the womb, willing to contain the force until the
timing is right for release and then letting the arrow fly, expressing its yang qualities.

The alchemist's mirror

If we turn the bow on its side, we see that it now becomes a vessel or cup containing fluid which creates a mirror-like surface
reflecting anything that looks within. For the alchemist, the bow
or cup represents a container of focused consciousness in which
magic and transformation can occur. The fluid, often represented
by the element of water, captures the image of what needs to be
manifest upon its mirror-like surface and absorbs the light energy,
with its image, into the fluid.

It is easy to see that the more stable and clear the surface of
the fluid, the more exact will be the representation. However, if
the surface contains ripples (caused by fear), is misty (caused by
anger), or is iced over (seen in depression), then the manifestation will lack congruency with the original. However, nothing is
ever lost, for when this happens it allows the alchemist to recognize the problem and make fine adjustments until there is a perfect match between thought and reality and between our inner
and outer worlds and, in this way, we come to *know ourselves.*

In a similar way to the bow becoming a cup or vessel, so the arrow is also seen as the serpent or wand of power. You will recognize that the sexual organs are a reflection of the bow and arrow although only an echo of the spiritualized cup and wand. As we move from the exoteric appreciation to the esoteric, the focus of the serpent no longer looks outwards towards an external target, but turns inwards and dives into the fluid-filled vessel, drawn in by the fluid itself: *fire on water*.

The serpent's fire power of transformation now brings to life the image held within the fluid while sacrificing itself to the process. This manifested form is then expelled into the physical world by the bow/vessel as crystallized light, reflecting the element earth. To complete the circle, when the time is right, dematerialization occurs, with the water dissolving the now wisdom-laden crystal back into itself. Here it awaits the fire power of the arrow which, with the aid of air, once again sacrifices itself to transform the wisdom into Universal light consciousness.

Alchemy involves the sacred marriage between force and focus until we reach the state of presence and the divine Eye of consciousness is revealed.

When serpent and fluid first meet to bring light into form, we see the shape of a semi-circle with a single line. However, when the second transformation occurs an equilateral cross within a circle is revealed, representing our ultimate goal, to merge the Self within the Source.

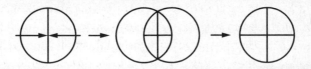

The Rose Cross

The rose cross

This same symbol (the equilateral cross within the circle) has been known as the Dew Cup of Fire and the cup of the fiery waters, descriptions from the past associated with menstrual flow and the power that is known to be present in a woman at this time. In ancient cultures, a woman would journey within, transcending time and space and tapping into the eternal power of Shakti, so as to maintain the connection to the Source for the group's spiritual survival.

As the position of women changed within society, other ways were found to maintain the spiritual link, such as through the ingestion of a white powder called *fire stone* which is currently known as *high-spin gold*. This gold stimulates the production of the hormones from the pineal gland which are similar to those found in the menstruating woman and hence with the potential to extend life, gain inter-dimensional awareness and produce excellent health. It is interesting to note that the practice of Qi Gong has been seen to have an analogous effect but it is only with gold that the state of wellness is maintained without stressing the adrenal glands.

It's no wonder that gold has always been seen to be more valuable than money and, exoterically, many are now interested to see if they can achieve this level of alchemical transformation merely by ingesting this metal. However, as always, we are seeking an external quick fix which will fail unless we prepare the crucible of alchemy which is the electro-physical form.

If we return to Eastern text, it is believed that only by refining and stabilizing our force and focus through the energy systems of our body and in particular the chakras will we eventually achieve the state of *loving presence*, when heart and mind meet in the area of the third eye. Then, using the breath, we unite this energy with that drawn in through the top of the crown to meet in the pineal gland. Such a union has a similar effect to the ingestion of high-spin gold, physically producing increased levels of melatonin but spiritually moving us to spaces of non-locality and union.

* * *

Stabilizing our intention

Many energies act upon our force and focus with those that are unbridled, such as fear, anger, shame and guilt, causing the focus to become scattered and the force to be compromised. The goal of the alchemist is to refine his/her inner force until it represents a *coherent laser-like energy*, and concentrate the inner focus until a state of *stillness* is reached.

Force = Power = How the activity will proceed = The energy behind the action

Focus = Attention = What is the purpose = Reflects the theme of the action

Perception = Personality/filters = Where the activity will take place = The scene

This same trinity is repeated in many other esoteric studies such as *astrology*:

Force = Planets = Motivating energy

Focus = Signs = Areas of attention

Perception = Houses = Arena or stage

and *numerology*:

Force = Action number = Birth date = Motivating energy

Focus = Combination of vowels and consonants
= Destiny number = Area of attention

Perception = Consonants
= Personality number = Outer world $\Big\}$ *Together they*
Vowels = Soul number *form the arena*
= Inner world

Each aspect of the trinity is important and any changes to one will influence the activity of the others. However the key is through our perceptions (the circumstances of this incarnation), for these were chosen by the soul to reveal aspects of itself that are still hidden and where invaluable sources of light energy and consciousness are waiting to be liberated. It is via the creative cycle and our willingness to know ourselves more fully, that we generate light energy which heightens consciousness and exposes new areas to focus our attention.

Let's look at some of the general variations that could affect our intention:

Too little focus

Imagine the damage that could occur if the archer mustered up all his/her strength and then fired aimlessly without focus. This happens all the time when we express a great desire to do something but then have no idea which direction to take or contradict the decision by immediately issuing a separate, unspoken thought: *"I really want a new relationship…but I actually prefer not to have my life disrupted by someone else's needs!"* Guess which one wins?

Focus demands us to be clear and honest and avoid speaking with *forked tongue,* asking:

"What do I really want? What fears arise at that suggestion and are those fears attached to old, outdated beliefs or are they realistic in the moment?"

It's so easy to find ourselves saying and doing the "right" thing to avoid attracting disapproval or rejection, rather than following our own truth. So often we use the excuse of not knowing what to do rather than confront a loved one with the need for change or with an opposing opinion, choosing to reject our own inner urges rather than be rejected by someone else.

In fact, if you've ever lived with someone who won't make a decision for fear of getting it wrong or having to commit to their choices, it can be very draining:

"What do you want to do today?"

" I don't mind; whatever you want is fine."

Later that evening, after many long sighs and silences you hear:

" I was miserable all day; why can't we do something I want to do sometimes!"

Choosing a focus and holding our aim demands us to take responsibility for our choices and not hide behind other people. What we have to decide is what is real to us and follow that truth as close as we can, however it appears to the rest of the world.

Sometimes, despite a willingness to step forward, we truly don't know what we want, so here are some suggestions to move the process forward:

* *If money were no object and you knew you couldn't fail, what would you do?*

* *In what situations does your heart sing?*

Remember times when your heart has been filled with joy or happiness and anchor the feeling in your body. Now ask: *"Is the same feeling present in your current circumstances?"* and if not, *"Can you instill a little of that energy into these situations and make a difference?"* If the answers are, *"No, No,"* you seriously need to rethink your plan and ask if your heart and mind are focused on your soul's purpose or are you still fulfilling the expectations of others.

* *Knowing that this may not be your final goal, what next step needs to be taken right now?*

Trying to climb Mount Everest before practicing on the foothills is one of the surest ways of sabotaging our efforts. On many occasions, opportunities arise that are stepping stones to the larger picture, and it's wise to follow this path rather than hanging on doggedly to unrealistic expectations which inevitably will lead to disappointment.

* *If you knew you would be loved whatever you did, what would you do?*

So often we fail to make a plan, as we're convinced that if we follow through on it change will be required which will adversely affect the lives of others, leading to repercussions towards us. But what if whatever you chose to do would be accepted and appreciated by others and you would still be loved?

* *Don't lean too heavily on the belief that "God will provide," and that, "It will all work out in the end."*

What is certain is that something will manifest but it may not be what you expect! Many women wait for ever for the knight in shining armor to appear on his brilliant white steed, ignoring the soul mate who arrives in his battered old car, jeans and tee-shirt. What your soul may need is not always what your ego wants!

As a wise man said to me, "Your responsibility is to make your way to the door and prepare yourself for the journey and then with humility wait patiently for the right time to pass through the doorway."

* *So set an intention that cannot fail such as:*

Let Divine Order and Divine Love work out

May I live out my Soul's Incarnation

Thy Will not my Will

Let my Soul's Purpose and Potential be Fulfilled

... and then let the arrow fly!

Too much focus

Then there are those who are so convinced they know exactly where they are going that they will never consider another option. If in the end they find themselves facing a brick wall, they will have the audacity to manipulate the situation by blaming the wall for being in the wrong place!

It's only through flexibility and open-mindedness that we can truly follow the path of the soul. To do this, we need to hone our intuitive skills so that we're able to pick up the subtle nuances that may indicate that it's time to let go of our "five-year plan" in favor of something that is a more perfect match for the rhythm of our soul. I have found that the most meaningful opportunities that moved me from one level of consciousness to the next, often appeared out of the blue and not from detailed planning.

In my experience, many of those who maintain such strict calendars are those who have fears around being out of control, of failing, facing the unknown unprepared, or feeling insecure. They are often thinkers or over-analyzers turning every little detail over in their mind before committing to an action. However, what may appear like a secure haven can become a prison inhibiting the natural nurturing of the soul which occurs through flexibility, connection, wonderment and by allowing spontaneity into our life. True control comes from having the courage to open the doors and let your light be seen as you give it the opportunity to grow from within.

So here's a very paradoxical suggestion:

Hold firm on the focus of your aim while being prepared to change it at a moment's notice!

Too little force

Next we meet the archer whose aim is true but whose strength is weak and, on releasing their arrow, it falls limply to the ground. The obvious answer is to sign them up at a local gym but there may be other reasons why their muscles failed to develop, including the lack of encouragement and nurturing of ideas and dreams during their early life. When someone receives constant criticism when young, they either use that negative force to strengthen their soul muscles, or they simply give up, causing the muscles of self-will to atrophy.

It then takes time and effort to restore strength, for negative messages become embedded in the framework of the individual and often need to be expelled first before further progress can be made. This may involve a period of therapy such as hypnotherapy or EMDR, which allow old patterns of belief to be dismantled so that the individual can create a new paradigm of self-awareness. At the same time, it helps to strengthen the physical muscles through martial arts, outdoor pursuits or physical exercise, as this entrains the mind into a new sense of inner focus and power. Whichever route is taken, the objective is to nurture the spiritual muscles back to health through activities that give soul pleasure, self-approval and increased self-confidence.

Once the fire is stoked in the basement and begins to rise along the spine then the archer's strength will be known and cannot fail.

Too much force

And finally we meet the archer who is unable to control their own strength and whose arrow not only hits the mark but practically destroys the target. The ability to master one's energy is an essential part of our journey on this Earth so that eventually we will find ourselves using *minimal effort for maximum effect*.

In particular, the archer needs to learn how to master his/her emotions as these powerful forces can be used to support the soul's journey or destroy it and hence:

Fear can excite, causing an adrenaline drive that gives us the courage to perform

Or it can paralyze our actions, leading to lack of strength and lack of focus

Anger can direct attention, leading to assertion and inner commitment

Or can burn out of control, destroying all that get in its way

Sadness can allow an individual to release ties that no longer serve the soul

Or can become all consuming, leading to lack of discernment and increasing depression

Happiness can bring joy and connection to any situation

Or can obliterate the truth when harmony and positivity are sought at any cost

Mastery comes through experiencing both sides of the emotional story and finding a middle way. Just as too little force emerges from lack of encouragement and criticism, it's not uncommon for those with excessive passion or energy to also be driven by a sense of inadequacy, carefully hidden by their anger against injustice, a desire to help the underdog, the willingness to take on other people's responsibilities and their martyr complex that revels in death rather than living a life as a humiliated failure.

The only problem for these *warriors* is that their passion can cause mist to form over their lenses, causing them to fail to assess the situation clearly with a rational mind and often do more harm than good in the long term. Many wars have been started and sustained by warrior individuals whose initial response was altruistic but who then used the battle to fulfill their own crusade. Investing so much energy into the cause they demand a result that matches their investment and become deeply wounded or angry when this does not manifest:

"After all I've done for you, I expected more for my efforts; you disappoint me!"

Passion and desire without wisdom is old Atlantean energy emerging from the solar plexus but is still used today as a powerful tool to motivate individuals. Such energy goads the recipient beyond their fear into a state of anger or aggression, motivating them beyond their paralyzed self. However, in this present Age,we are being asked to calm such passion and find a place for sound reasoning and consideration of all truths before action, drawing us towards a more peaceful future.

Chapter Eight

Becoming Present: Living in the Now

The most perfect expression of poise for the archers who await their shot, is when focus and force are stable, and is found within the state of *presence*. This is a place where fear has been transformed into love and we find ourselves focused on the moment within streams of expansive consciousness.

We are all and no-thing

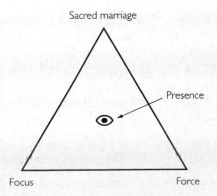

Being present offers us:

* peace and stillness of heart and mind

* an inner strength as we commit fully to ourselves

* a true centeredness

* being "rounded" rather than "grounded"

* no prejudgment, biases, expectations (no history from the past or agenda for the future)

* being seen and known for who we are now

* taking nothing for granted; accepting everything as a moment of gratitude

* openness and the power of vulnerability

* the potential for magic and transformation

* ecstasy and bliss; being one with the experience

* coherence and resonance with the now

In practical terms, being present brings:

* greater self-confidence

* enhanced connection with others linked to a deeper level of trust

* a receptive place for expansion and creativity

* expanded clarity

* honest interactions and willingness to be vulnerable

* maximal effect with minimal effort, reducing unwanted dissipation of energy

* inner strength rather than relying on logic, power games, emotional tricks or adrenaline instinct to drive actions

✳ a deeper connection to the self, others, all life forms and the Creative Energy

✳ greater desire to make conscious choices and take responsibility rather than looking for others to blame.

When we are present we're able to reach our full potential as a multi-dimensional being

* * *

To be present and live in the *Now* is to live on the edge of chaos which is the doorway into other dimensions and the full spectrum of possibilities available to us. Yet, it requires strength and stability of heart, mind and body to hold this space, and many lose their balance, being swept out to sea, or flounder on the sands or amongst the rocks, unable to free themselves. It is by anchoring ourselves in the worlds above, below and within (and knowing that there is no separation) that we develop firm roots of belonging and can withstand any change.

Being present or in the Now requires still, quiet strength and;

Is a doorway into inter-dimensional consciousness

...Is the site of true intention

...Is a place of magic and transformation

...and demands us to take responsibility for our lives.

One of the safest ways to live on the edge of chaos is through the creation of the vesica piscis. This is the perfect place for presence to exist, for here opposites have been brought together in the name of love, respecting all views and denying none. Here, there is no tension, for in essence there is no separation.

So why is being present such a challenge?

To Be Present is to Truly Know Ourselves and therefore, on some level, to Know God.

Historically, such awareness has not always been encouraged, for if we can reach this place of presence on our own and navigate our journey from that place, we have no need for an intermediary as we now have direct contact with the Source. Meditation is a perfect vehicle through which to find this space although not all disciplines achieve the result, for some, unfortunately, only encourage further disassociation.

Other than this, for relatively inexplicable reasons, *smoky mirrors* of perception were created lifetimes ago, distorting our vision much as a scratch on the lens of your glasses or a smear on the window glass would influence how you viewed the world. These mirrors caused us to become disconnected from reality and the sense of true presence, leading to innumerable fears which are a natural phenomenon in the face of separation. With no sense of certainty, the fears soon became the directors of reality around which we created a drama, causing us to become further lost in the smoky mirror.

Now every time we attempt to see beyond the distortions and return to the present, old fears arise tempting us to stay in the illusion. These include:

* fear of change, pain, the unknown

* fear of upsetting or hurting others

* fear of criticism

* fear of annihilation and a state of non-existence

* fear of being seen as uncaring as we disconnect from the dramas of others

* fear of being out of control especially when, in the past, playing power games, being fear-driven or pursuing intellect, have provided unrealistic levels of security

* fear of insanity, chaos and confusion

* fear that we may not like the reality that exists within the Now, preferring the illusion!

* fear that others will view us as unaccomplished or unsuccessful in the outer world as most of the work is inner

* fear of having to commit to our own journey when we've avoided this successfully for so long!

Avoidance patterns or addictions

To maintain the drama, we create patterns of avoidance and disconnection to re-enforce a belief that we're in control of what feels, in essence, a very uncertain reality: *"As long as I worry/work hard/exercise/eat/smoke, I'm in control."*

On a psychological and physiological level many of these avoidance patterns were originally designed as strategies to numb the individual to the immediate effects of **pain, confusion** and **fear**, just as a cell will move away from anything that threatens its survival. However on a soul level, there is a limit to how long it's healthy to stay numb, for when we disassociate we leave our body fairly unprotected and unfocused, allowing instinctual behaviors to run the show. In other words, we live purely on survival instincts, which are expensive in terms of their energy loss and do little to assure nurturing and growth for the soul.

And since the energy return on such fear-based habits is minimal, there is a need to continually repeat the pattern to achieve any kind of satisfaction. Hence, we become addicted to maintaining the activity, which monopolizes our attention and restricts our opportunity to seek more effective energy sources from within our being.

Any addiction limits the potential for full realization of the Soul, forcing the individual to live in a man-made box of rules and regulations just to survive.

And what's an addiction? I was taught that if we were unable to stop a habit for two weeks, we're addicted; for some not worrying for two minutes is hard!

Before we review some of the wonderful methods available to avoid living in the present, perhaps you would like to make your own list.

Then compare it with some of the methods listed below which include:

* preoccupied and anxious about the future: the *Worrier*

* living with constant guilt and regrets from the past: the *Guilt Tripper*

* being a *slave to work or projects* (workaholic) "busy being busy"; *no time for living!*

* the proverbial *Victim*: always provoking confrontation, pity, resentment and isolation

* abuse of drugs (legal and illegal), alcohol, gambling, smoking, food, chocolate and sex

* excessive interest in television, the computer, internet, telephone conversations, books and shopping

* overly serious, or the opposite, making light of every aspect of life

* controlling one's world through criticism, cynicism and skepticism

* overly responsible for everybody: the *Martyr*

* living other people's lives in the name of caring, teaching, advising, "knowing what's best": the *Controller*, avoiding contact with one's own needs

* introversion, aloofness and avoiding intimacy: the *Avoider*

* constantly talking: aversion to silence

* obsessive activity to avoid death and the ageing process, both of which are inevitable! Those who fear death need to *start living now*!

* over-analytical, always asking questions (never listening to the answers), living in the head, avoiding spontaneity

* living a life that pleases others, the reactor, walking on egg shells, being good, dutiful and trying too hard to get it right: the *Pleaser*

* obsession with meditation, religion, New-Age dogmas or disciplines that encourage giving power away or leaving the body for an ethereal experience

* being a professional patient where dependency abounds

* excessive exercise, walking the dog or any hobby that demands obsessive attention

* falling asleep to avoid confrontation

* perfectionism and fault-finding where nothing will ever be right

* floating out of the body, day-dreaming, living in fantasy land: *"Sorry, were you saying something?"*

* being too busy saving the world to commit to oneself

* *"When I win the lottery..."* Living in the fantasy of the future.

Most of these methods allow us to remain safe in an unsure world and yet deprive us of a deeper connection not only with ourselves and our Creator but with the important people in our lives with whom we wish to share our love. For true intimacy is only available when we have the courage and willingness to take down our self-erected barricades and remove the heavy armor, and that will only happen when we agree to return home and take control of our own lives.

Coming home to the present…a true gift

So are you ready to return and regain your own power and authority over your own home, life and soul. Are you ready to be like a baby who, starting to walk, learns to trust their own sense of balance and courageously stands again after a fall. The baby doesn't sense failure when it tumbles but sees it as a learning experience that is going to liberate it from a state of dependency and helplessness.

Trust develops out of the right relationship between spirit and matter; it comes from unconditional love and not because someone tells you to trust! In other words, the more you are committed to allow your soul to manifest through your body and personality, the greater the trust and inner strength that develops. And the only way that is going to happen is when we turn fear into love, shame into acceptance, and apathy into joy, and then we are unstoppable!

Chapter Nine

The Liberation of Energy

Intention = Force + Focus

With presence as our goal and the desire to expand our inner force and focus to their highest potential, it's helpful to appreciate the history of our emotions and how they have changed over the Ages. Emotions are a powerful source of inner force or fuel, with each emotion vibrating at a different frequency dependent on its particular function within the creative cycle. Hence *fear* is an exciting or creative energy, *anger* moves us, helping us to make decisions, *happiness* fills us with joy and fulfillment, and *sadness* encourages us to release and dissolve.

And yet, over time, the frequencies have been subtly changed so that instead of always supporting the cycle they may actually cause paralysis or disharmony. In a similar way to the mutation of a gene causing the manufacture of an abnormal protein, so I believe that the mutated emotions can ultimately work against the soul rather than for it.

This may have occurred through abnormal suppression of an emotion, through its exaggerated use or from genetic manipulation that occurred many eons ago causing individuals to fail to establish their ability to maintain their own energy supply through the appropriate use of their emotions.

And yet, while feelings are still present at any level so is the pure form of the emotion, even if it is held in suspension awaiting release. Our goal is to locate, transform and harness those emotions so that the energy they hold can be used to enhance and strengthen the light body, creating an inner force that is coherent and strong. To do this we often need to take our focus and attention into areas of our life that may be dark or gray and where emotions exist that may be difficult to acknowledge or that have been festering for so many lifetimes.

But now is a great time to take your lamp of inner light into those darkened areas and start to spring clean, clearing those dusty webs whose true beauty has not be seen for a long time. There are no bad emotions, only those which over the years have become distorted. For remember, everything is part of the Greater Plan. Liberating the golden seed that sits within some of the most difficult emotions can produce greater light energy and consciousness than the individual has ever experienced before. Much has been said about fear and sadness and, yet, I believe one emotion that is often overlooked and yet sucks the life force out of the individual is shame, where, buried deep down inside, is the energy of sublime love.

THE SLOW DEATH OF SHAME

Twenty years ago, as I listened to a talk on shame, I thought; *"They're not talking about me; let's move on to the next subject."* Now I know differently. Shame is insidious; it creeps up on you and is one of the most detrimental energies to the progress of connection and remembering. Wherever you hold a secret, there is the possibility of shame, and that will greatly limit your self-expression. On many occasions, the shame isn't even part of your present-day history but emerges from past lives, the lives of your ancestors, your culture, religion, gender, or just from belonging to the human race. Wherever you are joined to an energy line that has absorbed humiliation, defeat or scorn, then you know shame somewhere in your cells.

No one escapes having to face shame, whether in their own life or through tapping into the collective history of mankind, including Masters, Saints and wise Elders. For to reach that state of consciousness requires the traveler to enter into all possible conscious states and to acknowledge them as if they were their own, recognizing that enlightenment does not judge but merely respects the different aspects of the great Ocean of Consciousness flowing through us all.

Such a Master would explain that we cannot know Divine love until we are willing to embrace the darkest facet of shame and *love the unlovable.* Only then will we release the seed of sublime love that waits within, similar to the transformation of the Ogre by the kiss of the Princess. When we can love that part of ourselves, there is no separation between us and the Divine. To attract such an energy into our life at this time takes great courage, but many are choosing this path in order to clear age-old patterns of suppression and hence raise consciousness to new levels of compassion and tolerance.

As we enter into the ancestral web we draw into our being areas of shame that are left unresolved, often known as the *family secret.* The Bible states that it takes at least three generations to clear these roots and that it cannot happen by merely choosing to cut the ties for, energetically, the shame persists. Wherever unresolved secrets of disgrace or humiliation reside, we will find ourselves stopping on a dime if we attempt to pass through the door to freedom without dealing with the issue. For, on a soul level, it is a reminder that here is a source of tremendous power waiting to be liberated.

In order to achieve this goal, we first need to acknowledge shame's presence which can be difficult as, unlike fear which emits high-energy sparks, the energy of shame is introverted, silent and well concealed. Of all the emotions there is nothing as powerful as shame to bring a person to their knees and cause them to shrink inside in an attempt to withdraw as far as possible from the source of humiliation and dishonor. Shame de-personalizes, causing the individual to truly believe they are unworthy of love, acceptance or even acknowledgement and rejecting anybody who offers a different opinion.

No wonder it's been used for hundreds of years as a means to control the masses by those who knew that the greatest fears of the human spirit are abandonment, annihilation and the sense of not belonging; all by-products of shame. Add to that the apparent rejection by your God in the face of unworthy thoughts or actions as taught in many religions and you create an individual whose every line of communication, nurturing and support is destroyed, causing them to slowly self-destruct similar to any cell that lacks those basic needs.

One of the best-known shames is *original sin* interpreted as the *fall of man* brought about by the sensual and persuasive nature of a woman. This well-spun myth has prevented billions from truly knowing themselves and hence denied them their own inner strength and inherent connection with the Source. One brilliant feat of disempowerment!

Shame as a power to control

It is hard for us to appreciate in our physical world that *energy generated by the human form is more highly valued spiritually* than any material or mineral wealth. In other words, one of the cost-effective forms of fuel is human power, especially from those who are young or in the flow of creativity. Energy stealing is happening all the time and is more successful when an individual is shamed, fearful or in despair, for then they will easily surrender their energy to the lowest bidder.

In order to keep this knowledge for the few, there has also been a tendency to play down any real value from universally available supplies of energy such as the four elements, the Nature Kingdoms, meditative practices and energy medicine which are all *natural restorative sources of fuel* for the human spirit. Imagine what would happen to the profits of many of the major corporations if the general population knew that these natural and inexpensive forms of energy were readily available to them and would enhance healthcare, transportation, communication and education. It's not from a lack of belief that research and interest is underdeveloped but because those who hold the keys to power would rather keep that information to themselves.

It is also rarely taught that energy management is a vital part of healthcare, especially for the vulnerable such as children and young women, for their energy is both extremely vital and exposed. As you will see on the section on energy stealing, if someone has not learnt to maintain their own fields and generate power when needed, they will resort to filling their energy tanks by taking from other people. The most effective method to achieve this is to cause the vulnerable individual to separate or disassociate from their core being much as one would flee from a house without securing the doors and windows first, leaving it wide open to burglary. Whereas both irrational fear and anger can lead to a scattering of the individual's energy field, shame and abuse, especially over a period of time, causes such low self-worth that there is a tendency to completely give up ownership of the fuel pile.

Energy stealing from vulnerable individuals has been practiced over thousands of years sometimes unintentionally but often through semi-conscious design. Whatever the reason, one person gains at the cost of another and the cost to the weaker of the two may be their life as the more delicate systems of immunity, hematology, endocrinology and neurology take the brunt of the power loss.

Shaming is widespread today with some modern-day methods including:

1. Providing women with a role model of motherhood that embraces the virgin birth while subtly suggesting any other practice is inadequate or immoral.

2. The creation of poorly-designed league or hierarchical tables within schools, hospitals and spiritual communities, inciting the notion that those at the top of the list are to be praised while those at the lower end are to be further shamed.

3. The exaggerated celebration of heroes, unconsciously highlighting that there can only be one winner and everybody else is a failure. In a similar way, any traumatic death can leave those who live with "survivor" guilt, carried as shame for years after.

4. Women forced to cover themselves in shame because of men's unmastered urges, even in modern societies.

5. Idealizing a way of living or mode of appearance that, in reality, is only available to the few but causes others to live in a world of fantasy or failure.

6. Showing contempt and cynicism towards anybody who thinks or acts differently and causing others to rally to the cynic's side for fear of becoming victim to such wrath. What pain someone must have personally suffered to be so contemptuous that they would want to strip another human being of their dignity.

7. Bullying; epidemic in many societies despite so called democratic processes. Every day in many western schools, at least 25 per cent of middle-school children are experiencing a degree of torment that seriously affects their physical or psychological well-being, leading them

to consider suicide, refuse to attend school or even resort to violent revenge.

Bullying is not confined to children for it is seen to be rife within the corporate world, occurring across the board with little consideration for gender, race or breed and often seeping into homes where those who are bullied, regain their self-esteem by shaming those who are weaker and less able to answer back, such as children, partners and animals.

To humiliate someone is to strip another human being of their self-respect and self-worth, robbing them of their power whether consciously or unconsciously.

I remember a participant in one of my groups saying that she could tolerate all manner of criticism from her mother until she heard the words, *"I'm disappointed in you,"* at which the daughter crumbled inside. Words such as these suggest that expectations were set but not fulfilled and there is no going back.

Every parent must remember times of watching their children perform on stage or on the sports field praying they remember their lines, do not play a wrong note or drop the ball. And in the event of any of these mishaps occurring, they pray that they have the compassion to celebrate the efforts and hear the disappointment without aggravating any humiliation.

Unfortunately, too many adults and children did not receive such support and are left with the scars, still remembering the words or facial expressions of those from whom they sought approval.

"Did you have to show me up...?"

"What's wrong with you?"

"Why didn't you try?"

"That's the last time I'll come and watch."

"I was so ashamed!"

With all these messages, it's little wonder that children give up trying to achieve or lose interest in subjects where they struggle. A woman aged 50 who had just proudly finished a master's program told me that at the age of 13 she had been top of her class and, with head held high, gave her report card to her father. He took one look and said, *"Well, after reaching the top, there's only one direction to go now!"* From that moment on she never took another exam until she had the courage to overcome her father's cynicism.

What could have happened to that father that he found it so hard to celebrate and acknowledge his daughter's success? What pain and humiliation must he have suffered to have reached such a level of skepticism and cynicism where he no longer felt connected to the hurt he inflicted upon her? Or was he aware of his actions but unable to break the cycle for fear of exposing his own deep wound inside?

It is so easy to shame others through our criticism, personal jibes and cheap jokes at the expense of another, and yet we are hurt when the same games are played in reverse. And what does it take to praise, encourage and love? It takes our ability to know that we ourselves are able to be loved, not just by outsiders nor an external God-figure, but by the most loving part of our inner being who knows and sees our every move and loves us more.

The shameful secret

Shame is insidious; it invades our blood, our cells and forces us to hide.

Wherever there are secrets there is shame...

And the more fear used to re-enforce the secret, the greater the shame.

As we enter this new Era of respect, honor and compassion there is no place for secretiveness, as telepathic communication and interconnectedness demands an openness of mind and heart. If we accept the desire to remember and find the parts of the self still folded, we can no longer actively maintain secret lives, whatever their purpose, otherwise we continue the game of shame.

Put another way, the willingness to be seen frees you to be yourself; the fact that many will not have the eyes to see, is not your problem. It's the attachment to the secret that is the problem not the secret itself:

"What do you gain by maintaining the mystery?"

This concept challenges those who have, for some reason, compartmentalized their life often creating a enigmatic, elite existence where they feel special while obscuring the feelings of inadequacy and invisibility that are present within their real world. Now they are forced to live in fear that one day someone will find the key to their mind and expose their humiliating secrets.

Of course on one level we're all special, totally unique, as our fingerprints prove and yet on another we are beautifully and easily connected to all life; it is this polarity that maintains an optimal state of well-being.

So a question to ask yourself is, "What secrets are hidden either in my life or within the family? Where does shame dwell?"

"I've nothing to hide," comes the rapid response, expressed with far too much bravado and suggesting that the door has been sealed with the cement of reason and justifiable belief, banishing those uncomfortable energies called feelings.

Our capacity to share something with others is based on our experiences and perceptions as to how this will be received by our family, friends, culture, religion or gender. Where the rules of the land or social norms are tight, any misdemeanor is out of bounds, driving the truth further into hiding. At other times, where tribal or familial loyalty is maintained through fear, it is seen as the duty of its members to maintain the secret at any cost. As I have observed many times where sexual abuse had continued unabated down through the generations, when one individual had the courage to confront the truth, freeing themselves and their children from the energy line.

Even in so-called developed, modern countries episodes of

shaming continue with lack of support, for the one who reveals the truth as seen in:

* The child who tells their mother of the abuse they are suffering and is told not to lie

* The teenager who is experiencing daily bullying and is advised to "toughen up" as it will make them a man

* The adult who shares their secret and is met with disbelief, shock or a rapid response to "fixing" the problem, which merely drives the shamed one further into their warren of despair.

It is so much easier to offer a tablet than to sit with someone else's shame...
...being present with compassion and without judgment is a gift .

Groups such as AA have done much to encourage the speaking and sharing of shame but there are many areas left untouched as I hear traveling the world:

* *The man who is so ashamed at losing his job after 25 years that he continues to dress for work each morning, catching the same train but spends the whole day walking the streets before he can return home in the evening, pretending that nothing has happened*

* *The woman who never got over the guilt of having had an abortion and believes this is the reason why she can't get pregnant now with a man she loves; this is her punishment*

* *The child who's ashamed of the confusing sexual feelings that arise during the incest with her uncle causing her to believe that indeed she is the sinner*

✳ *The boy, now a man, who was never "good enough" in the eyes of his father and, with such low self-esteem, seeks positions at work that leave him frustrated and bored but at least not a failure*

✳ *The man who had a one-night stand early in his marriage and remains as a prisoner 30 years later to a wife who will never let him forget*

✳ *The woman who never forgets the birthday of the child she gave away and the shame of yielding to a man who threatened to leave unless she consented to unprotected sex*

✳ *The secret drinkers, especially women who only drink alone, attempting to convince themselves that they are on top of the problem and nobody knows*

✳ *The family who live in fear of anybody knowing what happens within the confines of their home, the physical, mental or sexual abuse, the gambling, the madness, the alcohol or drug addiction. For the "sake of the family" this is kept from the outside world*

✳ *The child who feels "dirty" when he's touched inappropriately by someone who should know better and yet feels powerless to do anything, causing him to feel more shame at his weakness and fear*

✳ *The men and women constantly shamed at work for the way they talk, look, think or dress and then shamed further as it's all done in the name of humor: "Can't you take a joke? You're far too sensitive!" When they attempt to retaliate, it merely fuels the fire for more jibes and attention*

✳ *The men and women shamed in front of neighbors by their partners: "Don't listen to him/her, he/she doesn't have a clue." "Typical of them to arrive late, and look at the way they're dressed."*

* *The family with a child or adult who acts in a manner that doesn't fit into the social norms and knowing that everybody is looking; what courage to walk freely and with such compassion.*

Transforming shame into love

In my opinion shame and humiliation can never be treated by further shaming, despite attempts to "jolt" the person out of their misery. All that happens is that there is further disassociation and separation in an attempt by the individual to avoid additional disapproval and pain. Many become *pleasers* eager to be acknowledged at the cost of their true feelings, their energy supply and soul's truth.

What is needed is compassion, not pity, and appropriate support. Comments such as:

* *A little criticism is good for you; it will harden you up*

* *I had to go through it; it makes you stronger in the long run (if they survive)*

* *It's your karma*

* *Surely that didn't bother you (which merely deepens the shame)*

merely exacerbate the problem and heighten the sense of isolation.

On many occasions shame surrounds a situation that, at the time, was dealt with in the best way possible but still left its mark. On other occasions, it is the judgment by others that causes the scar, especially when their opinion was sought and valued. Healing occurs through acceptance and love of that part of ourselves we believe is unlovable.

As we commit to remembering and integrating all those parts still in the shadows, deep-seated shame will often emerge as a catalyst for transformation and reconnection. Although we may seek forgiveness from others or absolution for our thoughts or actions, unless we are taught to do the same for ourselves without an intermediary, we are left just as powerless.

During a particularly traumatic time in my inner journey, I came to appreciate that healing would only occur when I had the courage to meet the part of me where pain almost caused me to cry out in despair. I visualized myself descending into a deep dark well of my psyche where, curled up in a corner almost without true form, was an image that I knew instinctively as my *shamed one.*

It seemed to cower in my presence, trying to merge into the wall to escape my attention and was shocked when I spoke to it directly. *"I see you, I know you and accept you as a precious part of me. What can I do to help you in your pain?"* Minutes went by before a reply came in a very quiet voice, *"Love me in all my shame,"* and, instantly, I felt my heart open and waves of love flow forth embracing this courageous part of myself. I knew then that there was nothing I could do or say that couldn't be met with such love. Instantly, I experienced a depth of forgiveness that reverberated deep within my soul, and I came to understand that true forgiveness occurs not in the head as an idea but on a psychocellular level which can never be undone.

So what part of you holds shame, and are you ready to love the unlovable?
For, in truth, shame holds the potential for Eternal Love.

In that moment, I was brought to a sense of inner peace, unknown until then, and knew instinctively that the particular type of shame or knot within my family line had been cleared, releasing all those who had been bound by it whether still alive or dead. I also came to understand that by transforming my own shame at the deepest level possible, I had helped to raise the vibration of the energy line of *Love* that passed through me and simultaneously reduced the shame of others all around the world.

When we are willing to truly do our own inner work, the results affect more individuals than just ourselves.

Philip tells a very similar story. During a group visualization, he opened a door at the end of a corridor only to hear a heart-wrenching wail on the other side. Shutting the door quickly, it took him a few days to have the courage to repeat the process and to start a dialogue with the being who cowered darkly in the corner.

He was told that he had abandoned this part of himself years ago because of the displeasure it caused his father and now its only opportunity to be heard was when he drank a little too much wine, loosening his tongue. On further questioning, this dark sub-personality spoke of its ability to see beyond the masks of other people, often into their pain, a talent unappreciated by Philip's father, hence the banishment.

Over the weeks, Philip gained the confidence of this side of himself and one day on entering the hidden room he was surprised and delighted to see the cowering figure had turned into the most beautiful woman, his anima and intuitive side of his nature, which he spontaneously embraced and felt a wholeness that, for him, was a completely new experience.

✳ ✳ ✳

Shame offers us the opportunity to experience a level of love and light that is invaluable on the soul's journey towards self-realization. Many attempt to bypass this particular doorway, saying with scorn, *"But that's so unspiritual."* And yet, it is here that true spiritual work takes place reflected in the path of many enlightened beings who we so revere. It takes courage to look within and embrace this quivering mass but, when we do, we are rewarded with one of the most abundant outpourings of compassion we will ever know, annihilating any fear of being exposed or need to hide. Immediately, the walls of inadequacy start to fall and our light energy shines forth for all to see.

FEAR AND ANXIETY

There is no place for fear

When I heard these words, spoken by a wise Elder of the
Hawaiian tradition, my immediate thought was that he'd lived a
life of naivety on these idyllic islands and obviously didn't know
the real world. But then I saw his body, scarred by the effects of
being wounded in separate wars and I said to myself, *"What do
I know of fear?"* I heard him speak of his father sending him out
on his "vision quest" at the age of 12 with a one-way ticket and
how he had reached his present position amongst his people
through guts, determination, humor and great inner wisdom. He
had learnt to face his own fears and find compassion for them
so that they no longer directed his life, and so he could use their
energy for creativity and growth rather than false protection or
even destruction.

He added, *"Fear always separates us from our true self and makes
us vulnerable to the whims of others; it is only through compassion for all parts of ourselves that we can free ourselves from the
bondage of fear."*

On one level, this powerful emotion is an instinctual energy providing us with the means to triumph over adversity. While on
another, it is a force that destabilizes our existence, making it
increasingly difficult to connect with what is real. Look at the many
actors, sports people and presenters who rely on this chemical
high to reach the peak of their performance or the bosses who
promote a level of anxiety so as to entice the most out of their
workers. And yet the down side is that, like any drug, the with-
drawal symptoms rob the individual of any rewards, forcing them
to seek another hit or to be left with continual floating anxiety.

At the same time, fear deprives us of the ability to act from a
place of wisdom, or experience soul nourishment, making it almost
impossible to work for the greater good, for it forces us to always

protect our own needs. And the saddest part of all is that, as fear drives us further and further from our inner core of Truth, we find ourselves trusting no one, including ourselves, and weaving webs of delusion, spinning one lie after another in an attempt to maintain a tenuous form of control. In the end, the only person who is fooled by the lies is their creator who is now unable to tell the truth or develop deep relationships as they have traveled so far from their core.

Through the disconnection that occurs as a result of fear we are unable to tap into the eternal source of power that is our birthright.

When we choose to face our fears and embrace the estranged parts of the self, an inner strength starts to develop and we are drawn to places that had previously held so much fear, only to find a warmth and comfort that had been missing for so long. This gives us the courage to *act not from fear but from love* and causes us to wonder how we ever got caught up in the rat race of fear when, from a spiritual point of view, we always knew that time, space and the material world don't exist except within our minds. This reminds us that:

There is always enough time, never-ending space and that all our soul needs are already met, somewhere in the Universe.

Several years ago, I was standing on the platform of an Underground station in London waiting for my train. It was March and hence the end of the UK tax year and there on the walls opposite were plastered advertisements entreating the reader to invest any extra money in various lucrative accounts each offering a better interest rate than the last. As I walked down the platform, I saw other advertisements promoting the latest in internet technology and telephone schemes. Galvanized by the trains that passed through the station, I felt my mind starting to race with questions such as,

"Have I invested my money wisely? Should I change my portfolio?

"Maybe I could get more services from another internet server?"

"Am I getting the best deal on my telephone calls?"

In my mind, I saw myself running up and down the platform, jumping on and off passing trains, frantic to "get it right" without any depth of thought as to whether I actually needed the product. Then suddenly in that moment I saw what was happening. I'd fed into a fear that, even though it didn't meet with my soul's beliefs, had managed to push all my buttons of self-doubt as well as touch the belief that someone else knew better. Instead of receiving the information in a rational manner and allowing it to enhance my own wisdom I had panicked, forgetting that fear can only take hold where doubt or separation from the Self already exist. Fear is an addiction, more powerful than most chemical drugs, and is used by the advertising world to sell their products and by the media to sell their propaganda.

But, like any addiction, it can be managed if we can just stop long enough to achieve an overview of the situation, often receiving invaluable support from those who have walked the same path. Through time and the ability to love and accept even those parts that hold low self-esteem and insecurity, the spaces where fear can enter begin to diminish and a new freedom is experienced.

Fear like shame holds the key to a deeper level of emotion if we have the courage to face it, releasing into our fuel tanks increasing quantities of vital energy in the name of excitement, enthusiasm and a love of life.

Facing the fear of losing what (you believe) gives you control

For the first few weeks of the sabbatical I took after leaving general practice, I walked around believing that I had a notice on my front saying, *"Out of work doctor; invalid member of society."* As I watched people leave for work in the morning and found myself shopping in the middle of the day, I slowly saw how much I had relied on my identity to bring meaning and acceptability to my life. I would meet those in full-time jobs who, challenged by my decision, would ask, *"Can you afford to make this move?"* and I would reply, *"I can't afford not to!"*

As we face our fears, we will often attract people or create situations in our life that will question our resolve, *"Are you sure you've made the right decision?"* It is not uncommon for such tests to come surprisingly from those who are dearest to us and from whom we are seeking support. But like physical muscles fortified at the gym, tests of the mind strengthen our mental muscles until we are certain that they can support the weight of our new direction.

So what do you fear losing?
What do you believe gives you a sense of being in control?

 ✳ *Partner, family, friends, children etc.*

 ✳ *Identity at work, within the family or society*

 ✳ *Evidence of security through wealth or possessions, including home, car, money in the bank, vacations or food on the table*

 ✳ *Proof that if I work, act or think a certain way all my needs will be met*

 ✳ *Being loved*

 ✳ *Health; what does that mean?*

 ✳ *Sanity*

 ✳ *Peace and harmony*

 ✳ *Freedom; is there a cost?*

 ✳ *Other people's approval. Etc.*

They are all saying, *"If I lose any one of these I am sent into a spiral of fear and helplessness."* Watch out, because their presence in your life is more tenuous than you think and, while you fear losing them, you may attract towards you something that will challenge your dependence. It isn't that you shouldn't enjoy money, friendships etc., but your fear-based attachment to them is a liability to the soul's growth.

You will always be vulnerable and drained of energy when your survival or security is based on something that you fear losing. Once you relinquish your dependence on your most precious possession then you are surrounded by it in abundance.

True freedom for the soul comes when there is nothing to lose, for you have everything and need nothing.

Fear connected to change

The one thing in life that is certain is change; it's just a matter of when and how.
Each breath we take draws in a new source of air.
Every encounter changes us for ever.
You're not the same person as you were a minute ago.

As we open our hearts and minds to remembering and drawing our energies of force and focus into balance, we are often faced with the need to change old ways and step into a new mode of life. Despite the fact that on some level we invited this change, its presence can throw us into a state of panic as we're suddenly faced with the unknown, frantically searching for the coping mechanisms stored within our memory banks that have served us in the past. On other occasions, we simply freeze at the prospect of change, numbing ourselves to the inevitable and trying desperately to hold back the tide and pretend nothing is happening.

And yet there are times when we openly welcome change, seeking its warm embrace as we would a new and exciting lover, ready to leave behind beliefs, situations or relationships that no longer serve our soul or that have run their course. But be clear, not all change asks us to leave something or someone. Often, it entices us to draw closer, reconnect on a deeper level, move beyond our fears and embrace new aspects of our being as yet untested. For many, this concept of change is far more challenging and formidable than departure.

Change is not the enemy, it is a friend that moves us towards a greater understanding of ourselves, a deeper re-membering and self-knowing.

Let us explore a few of the common fears that arise at the thought of change:

* *Fear of isolation, rejection and abandonment*

* *Fear of guilt and hurting those we love*

There are no slick solutions to the dilemmas above, for self-individualization is asking us to metaphorically step out alone and, in truth, others may not understand and may feel hurt but there are four rules to keep in mind:

Will my actions bring greater soul growth and soul expansion?
Will this ultimately benefit the group or the tribe?
What role model do I want to leave to my children and grand-children?
Is it better to be rejected than reject my own inner urgings?

Guilt is a quality that has been grossly overplayed and commonly acts as an excuse rather than the means to change patterns of a lifetime; *"If only I had been a better mother/father/friend/therapist...this wouldn't have happened."* Don't kid yourself, you're not that powerful!

* *Fear of failure*

For many, failure is perceived as bringing further humiliation to an already fragile ego and hence the individual holds onto the belief that, *"If I don't try, I can't fail."* Yet the other face is, *"What if I never try? What then is failure?"*

Too many people die with regret over a relatively simple matter that, through the years, has developed into an almost insurmountable challenge, such as:

* saying; "I love you," to a parent, wayward child or
  even ourselves

* being honest about an issue where, in the past,
  maintenance of harmony was more important than
  the truth

* saying, "I'm sorry, I was wrong," especially where we
  have to lay aside pride or a victim consciousness

* attempting something that has always evoked fear and
  even though the results may be limited gaining real
  pleasure from the courageous effort

* taking time out to play, make space for friends and
  family, or being present to other people's joys
  and anguish

* acting in a manner that expresses the authentic self
  and not the one that hides behind limiting rules
  prefixed by should, must, ought, can't and got to

What regret is ready to be healed now?

Failure is a quality of small eyes emerging from small minds
and doesn't exist as a concept in the consciousness of the
divine creative process.

**We cannot fail the experience but only
fail to grow from it.**

* Fear of success

Both failure and success have the potential to rock the boat
in the greater scheme of things, starting with friends and
family, with the inner message, *"What if I'm more
successful than my father or my closest friend?"* Here

success is seen as a disadvantage that has the potential to cause embarrassment and ruin a comfortable relationship. So since **we** feel ill at ease, we often try and persuade the other person to "become successful" so we grow alongside without affecting the status quo.

Of course, the other person is usually perfectly happy where they are and we are the **only** person with a problem. Success requires us to be seen and heard and rejoice in our achievements and hence:

Let the work do the work
Get out of your own way
Transform success into fulfillment and see it as soul nourishment
Remember that we all have different paths and what may be success to one may not be recorded as such by another
See success as soul contentment and as your small contribution to Universal Consciousness

✳ *Fear of being out of control*

✳ *Fear of the unknown*

"Can you guarantee me that I will never have to suffer, be responsible, live in doubt and I will always know happiness?"
"No, because why would you want those assurances if you are here to grow into a fully conscious being?"

Life was never meant to be a static state where everything was ordered and everything was known. We are here to add to the pool of consciousness through our actions, each time entering with a sense of innocence while maintaining our link to wisdom. The task of the alchemist is to move fearlessly from structure to chaos and then back to structure, passing through the core of stability in the center, the edge of chaos.

In essence, the only way to grow spiritually, know ourselves, or be of service, is to embrace the sense of being out of control just as the caterpillar knows that by entering the cocoon and abandoning the security of his many legs, he is being offered the abundant freedom which is the butterfly. It seems ironical that someone should attempt to stay secure through their little ego, when so much more is being offered.

Trust enables us to step through the doorway although this is not a trust based on bargaining rites, promises and the fact that because of your faith you will be safe. The only trust that matters is in the process, i.e. *that something will change.* How it will affect you, and whether during the journey your soul will be enhanced, is the risk we take. Our spirit family and guides can reveal the path but they cannot move us to take the next step. This is for three reasons:

* The value of the journey into consciousness is based on that first step.

* We have free will and nobody can interfere with that...And I mean nobody.

* Those who guide us forfeit their own level of consciousness if they step in, especially when not appropriately requested, i.e. if we do not ask with an open heart and mind.

* * *

What we know is that:

> *When the fear of change*
> *is greater than the fear of staying where we are*
> *we will not change.*

In practical terms, it has clearly been shown in the field of cell biology that every cell has only two directions to move: either away from pain, or towards pleasure, whichever is the most compelling force. At our basic and most instinctual level, we are no different from the cells, so for successful change we must:

Create a perception of change that is pleasurable and then we'll move towards it.

One way of doing this comes from the arena of NLP (neuro-linguistic programming) where we remember a time when we felt confident and found pleasure in our activities, allowing the associated feelings to effuse the body and mind. Then, while maintaining the feelings within the body, we transport our awareness to the new situation, seeing it through the eyes of enjoyment and ease and overlaying old messages of fear with stronger and more impelling impulses. The final stage of the process is to anchor the new feelings into the body by placing a hand on a part of the body that needs to hear the message, re-enforcing its impact.

If all else fails, *change will happen anyway*, initiated by our higher self which lovingly loosens our fingers from the last remaining handhold and catches us when we fall.

It is not the change you make that matters but that you made the change.
The more conscious your choice to change, the greater the energy generated by such an activity.

Fear through the process of change
Listening to the messages from the Higher Self
Sometimes, its not always clear which path to take but when we learn to trust our intuition we soon know which paths **not** to take! A frequently told story is one that involves a telephone call where you agree to take part in a project that, at the time, sounds exactly what you're looking for. But, as you finish the call, you experience a dramatic sinking feeling and you hear a deep inner cry, screaming, *"No way!"*

This is followed commonly by symptoms that include shaking, anxiety, a feeling of being burdened, exhaustion, a desire for sweets or other comfort items, a sinking feeling in the pit of the stomach and the knowledge that you have to *get out of the situation fast!* And when you do have the courage to pick up the phone again and decline the offer or extricate yourself from the situation, waves of relief flood over you and you know you've made the right call.

Trusting this invaluable inner guide will save a lot of heart- and headache in the long run, although we often learn this lesson only after attempting to see the promise through to its conclusion, almost killing ourselves in the process.

The closer to change the louder the voice

As a wise man taught me: *"Fear will always try and trick you into believing that all it wants is your safety, when sometimes that safety denies the soul its potential."*

It's important to know that as we approach the door of transformation, there is often a small voice inside belonging to our little self that sees no reason to disturb the status quo and hence can become extremely vocal, shouting, *"No, you don't want to do this!"* I see this happen so often when people are in transition and when 99 per cent of them know they are making the right choice. But the one per cent that is still invested in the past and can see no reason to change, wants them to appreciate its concerns and the sacrifices it has made to keep them limited!

When a client in change tells me they feel increasingly anxious, I will secretly say, *"Good,"* because I know we're on the right track, and I work to reassure this one per cent voice that we appreciate its service but it's time to move on and perhaps it would like to take a short holiday while the transition occurs!

Fear as undirected creative energy

Anxiety also occurs as a result of undirected creative energy as we begin the turn that ultimately is going to take us in a new direction, because for a while we find ourselves free-floating without focus. Imagine driving down a road at 70 mph and then deciding to turn but with your foot still fully pressed on the gas pedal. The car would behave in a very similar manner to your body during an anxiety attack, shaking violently and screaming for you to release your foot from the pedal and continue in the old direction.

This is extremely common in those who live their life with focus and determination, never easing up long enough to take a deep breath and check in with their inner guidance. Hence it comes as a shock when, without warning, a deeper part of their consciousness decides; *"Time for a change; brake now!"* and the little self is thrown into a panic because not only was he/she taken by surprise but there is a feeling of being completely out of control.

The obvious solution is to attempt to return to the original track but surprisingly, when you look, that road has magically faded before your eyes and you're forced to acknowledge that the only thing you can do is to trust the inner driver and navigator who seem to have a plan outside your immediate comprehension. My first experience of this phenomenon was several years ago during a major change that involved my inner life as much as my outer. I found myself waking morning after morning with fear and anxiety that started in the pit of my stomach and radiated out with a voracity that didn't cease until it reached the top of my head and the tips of my toes.

I tried everything: praying, meditating, chanting, affirmations, deep breathing, listening to music and even standing on my head! All to no avail. The only thing that seemed to work was to become busy either in the office or around the home which I knew instinctively was self-defeating as it purely fed my addiction to action.

Then one morning, after several weeks of this disturbance and as I became more and more exhausted by what felt like a battle, I stopped and asked myself what I really feared. I had already thoroughly checked many of my fears and found them to be red herrings:

> *What if I don't make money?*
> *Can you make money by other means?*
> *Yes!*
> *So, that's not the problem.*
> *What if there's no security in the future?*
> *Has that ever happened in the past?*
> *No!*
> *So, that's not the problem.*
> *What if people abandon me for what I'm about to do ?*
> *Have they left in the past?*
> *No, they've always supported me.*
> *So, that's not the problem.*

And on and on I searched for the source of the fear.

Then out of the blue it dawned on me that what I feared was *fear itself.* I feared whether I would survive the effect fear had on my body and mind. I remembered times in my life when, on hearing news that was shocking and unexpected, I had taken the shock in through my solar plexus but then numbed myself to the impact, never truly expressing my deeper feelings. Now I was preparing myself once again to experience the unknown and the suppressed symptoms from the past were emerging in force similar to the markers of post-traumatic stress disorder.

I decided to face my demons and prepared myself through invoking help and support for my journey and surrounding myself in love and light. As I sat I asked that I should feel in my body all the sensations associated with my anxiety, and immediately I became flooded by waves of shaking, nausea, tingling in my fingers and toes and a craziness in my head of being out of control. But as the sensations continued, a buzz of exciting energy emerged from deep within and I knew that I was experiencing the opposite side of fear, pure creative energy and joy, for there was now nothing preventing me from receiving it. I felt as if I had found the elixir of life hidden within a tomb that could only be opened if I was brave enough to embrace my own fear.

I felt elated with a freedom from anxiety that I hadn't experienced for months, and reflected during the day that as therapists we often persuade clients to ignore or bypass their fear when, all the time, their very salvation is waiting within. However, I would not advise someone to sit with their fear until a place of stability had been reached so that they could maintain an observer role during the process.

Within days, I had a flash of a past life which enabled me to see and transform a thought pattern that I had carried, not just for one life, but for many. It coincided with the fact that when I was exhausted I would often say I felt *shattered*, never really understanding why I insisted on using this phrase even when I attempted to reframe it.

In this past life, I saw myself as a captain in the First World War serving in the trenches. Conditions were squalid and many of the regiment were dying as much from the effects of disease, malnutrition and the cold as from the weapons of war. It angered me to see thousands of soldiers dying with little progress being made and I felt that we were just pawns in a game played out by generals in their safe, dry headquarters miles from the front-line.

One day, I made a stand and accused my commanding officer of sending soldiers to their death purely at whim and without consideration for their lives or families at home. He accused me of cowardice and, feeling outraged, I said, "I'll show you," and, with no regard for caution, led my men over the top of the trenches into battle, seeing many of them instantly shot down and myself finally standing on a landmine where I was "shattered" and died.

I realized that since that time I blamed myself for not mastering my feelings and for allowing them to be the cause of so many deaths. I also realized that I was still fighting battles trying to save people from the clutches of death through my work as a doctor and by taking on the concerns of others as my private crusade.

Oh, what patterns we continue from one life to the next!

But I also knew enough about past lives to know I was being given the opportunity to change the future, and hence I returned, in meditation, to my soldier as he stood in the trenches before the fateful assault.

He now realized he had choices. He could continue fighting every crusade to prove himself or could choose forgiveness and allow the battle-weary warrior of many lives to find some peace.

He made his decision and started to walk between the mud-drenched walls and away from the battle. Laying down his gun, he vowed that he would find a new way of functioning which didn't involve defense or attack; as he took off his gas mask he knew that life was not worth living if he couldn't smell the sweet air of the morning; removing his heavy coat, he surrendered the need to sur-round himself with those things that failed to nurture his soul; tak-ing off his jacket with all its bravery medals, he knew that this was one of the most courageous events of his life: being true to himself; and as he removed his helmet and boots he felt the warm wind in his hair and the soft earth under his feet and knew he had returned from a death far more devastating than any physical loss, the death of part of himself. The past was over.

As I accepted the warrior into my core, I didn't abandon the importance of standing by my truth or of working together with others to create a better world but I did realize that destruction and separation are the only possible outcomes when fear and anger are my allies. Since then I have found a wiser and more objective manner of working with my warrior and the word "shat-tered" has completely faded from my vocabulary.

Chapter Ten

Maintaining Energy

ENERGY STEALING

Watch out there are vampires about!

This old-fashioned and well-tested way of acquiring energy without having to "do the work" involves finding someone who leaves their energy store unguarded either due to innocence or lack of appreciation of its value. It is a subject that I believe is not discussed adequately, partly because the problem is rife. We have probably all played both roles sometime during our life especially when vulnerable, fearful or experiencing low self-worth. Children and those who have a similar naive view of life are easy victims, as seen in the appalling instances of abuse and exploitation. It is unfortunately part of the human condition to take something that doesn't belong to us, often surreptitiously, and psychic or energy theft creates a greater karma than any physical crime.

The Ancient People describe *young souls* as those who build and create karma through such actions, *mature souls* as those who no longer accumulate karma, allowing others to live their lives as long as it doesn't involve them and *old souls* as those unaffected by the actions of others.

Story

The Great Buddhist saint Nagarjuna moved around naked except for a loin cloth and, incongruously, a golden begging bowl gifted to him by the King who was his disciple. One night he was about to lie down when he saw a thief lurking in the shadows. *"Here, take this,"* he said, handing the bowl to the man, *"then you won't disturb me when I'm asleep."*

The thief eagerly grabbed the bowl and ran off – only to return the following morning with a request: *"When you gave me this bowl so freely last night you made me feel poor. Teach me to acquire the riches that made this light-hearted detachment possible."*

(from *The Heart of the Enlightened* by Anthony De Mello)

Walking into the sacred space of another person and removing something that is not your property for your personal gain mirrors the actions of physical burglary, sexual abuse and the acquisition of land that is already inhabited by others. Such action is strongly allied to **power games** which, linked mainly to the lower three chakras, are often played by those who have forgotten how to generate their own energy or who have lost their spiritual connection to the Source. The thief, often with their own low self-esteem, feelings of inadequacy and social isolation, seeks someone with:

* poor boundaries

* poor self-worth

* need for approval or acknowledgement

* desire for harmony at any cost

* need to be liked or needed

* passion to help, rescue, serve or change others

* feelings of insecurity within the tribe, group, family in
  which they live or work

...or anybody with any kind of fear, including that of humiliation,
inadequacy, rejection, abandonment, being out of control, going
crazy or of not being loved!

You can see why energy-stealing is rampant!

Without much effort, the thief has a ready source of energy without the need to commit to the important responsibility of maintaining their own supplies. The two main methods used to persuade the subject to release his/her energy, are through:

1. **Threats or bullying**
   "If you don't give me what I want I will..." focusing on
   the area of fear in the mind of the individual.

2. **Charm, persuasion or the offer of friendship** to a
   vulnerable person. *"I can see you're special and I know
   what you're going through. Let me help."*
   This grooming is often followed by flattery and even
   seductive sexual advances accompanied by words such
   as, *"I love being around you/in your energy. You're the
   only person who really cares; I feel so much
   stronger/brighter in your company."*

Fear or flattery work every time!

Other means of stealing energy include:

* Criticism, comparisons, one-upmanship, passive

aggression (charm hiding the anger), cynicism, ridicule *(Base or First chakra)*

* Refusal to receive, rejection of love, aloofness, avoidance, martyrdom. *"I'm fine, I'll cope, I'm strong," (Sacral or Second chakra)*

* Being a victim, helpless and creating guilt in others. *"I thought you were a good person but nobody can help me and its not my fault!"* The individual feeds on the energy of reaction, saying; *"You have failed me and my expectations and I'm not talking to you until you give me a little of your energy!" (Solar Plexus or Third chakra)*

* Refusal to be fully present to another person or rejecting or criticizing their qualities; lack of commitment and intimacy *(Heart or Fourth chakra)*

* Cutting through another's speech to gain attention, needing to tell a superior story to score, constantly asking questions rather than listening or insulting the other's intellect or memory, *"Don't you remember you said you would... You're not as intelligent as I thought you were," (Throat or Fifth chakra)*

A skilled vampire will be a psychic chameleon, able to read the moods and needs of another and quickly transform their posture, facial expressions and words to extract the most energy from their victim. We've all been taken in by such professionals who have little or no true depth of character but a wonderful array of elaborate costumes and, hence, are very convincing. Their expressions of hurt and anger or pleas for forgiveness appear and disappear with amazing speed followed by almost complete amnesia and denial that the exchange ever took place, leaving their subject confused and doubting their sanity.

During an unwanted invasion into your energy field it's not uncommon to physically experience someone's presence as a tingling, temperature change, tightening of muscles, draining of energy or thoughts within your head that do not belong to you. The first time I experienced this was when traveling in India visiting various ashrams. I found my mind being entered by a powerful force who demanded that I should tell my inner teachers to turn their allegiance to this particular guru. It all happened in seconds and I vehemently refused, but I saw how easy it is to allow someone to influence our thoughts causing us to "doubt our own mind."

I also recall a powerful Maori healer relating a story of a visit to a spiritual community where, even before the introductions had been made, three people had attempted to enter her base chakra and she had seen them off the "property" with a severe reprimand. At the time I was perhaps a little unsure of what she meant, until I had a similar experience a few months later, surprised by the audacity of some people! The energy thief often increases their supplies through continuous inappropriate physical touching although on many occasions the mere tone of the message whether via the internet or telephone can cause us to abandon our supplies.

There is one final group who I perceive as energy suckers, and these are people who have passed through the menopause, both men and women, and who have never acquired the ability to activate and maintain their own creative energy cycle. For women, the training of such maintenance is somewhat easier, for the menstrual cycle teaches them to receive the egg, nurture it to fruition and allow it to die if fertilization is not required that month. However, ultimately we all need to be able to take an idea from birth to death, for this is how we generate light energy. For people who, by the menopause, have never reached that level of fulfillment in their own life, physical and psychological symptoms of energy deprivation will start to appear until either the creative cycle is activated or the individual finds someone who is still young and vital which, in the case of men, is often a menstruating woman.

This is the reason why many marriages flounder when the partners reach their fifties or sixties and the *juice* fails to flow, exacerbated by our failure in the western world to value and appreciate the place of the elder in society. Hormone replacement is not the answer, for it acts purely on the surface while, beneath, the spiritual creative energy is still absent. Taking up a hobby or returning to a creative pursuit that you abandoned years ago is often the answer along with a readjustment in the relationship where both seek to inspire the inner being of the partner, rather than seeking energy from elsewhere.

* * *

It's often easier to give in to the vampire than to consciously resist and face the onslaught that follows. As with children who don't get what they want or who are caught sneaking another cookie from the jar, adults who fail to procure the energy they seek or whose actions are named, often react quite violently or sneak off to lick their wounds, muttering words of revenge. Like the four-year-old, they may hurl accusations that hurt but, unlike the child, there is more energy and venom behind the words and hence are harder to ignore.

Saying, *"No,"* is a tough call at any time but in the presence of a vampire, it needs to be accompanied by a psychic close down so that no further energy is leaked. Methods that help include:

* Strengthening the inner light through self-compassion, increasing self-esteem and standing firm

* Calling the individual on their behavior. For the most part, it is an unconscious act and your insight may allow them to change their patterns

* Choosing to master the emotions, for when they are uncontrolled they allow easy access for the thief to enter

* Surrounding yourself in white light or a rainbow-colored cloak from head to toe

* Imagining a solid gold door closing in front of the body, especially the lower chakras and asking that, *"Only those things in resonance with my soul pass through the door"*

* Placing oneself inside a golden pyramid with a golden floor and with light entering through the top, saying, *"All that is not good for my soul growth, please let it return to the source"*

* When bombarded with energy, **imagine** holding a mirror in front of the body with the reflective surface towards the other person and letting their energy reflect back to them

* As the *solar plexus* chakra picks up energy easily, crossing the arms across the upper abdomen affords protection

* Refusing to justify your feelings of ill-ease or distrust and asking that your request for distance, etc. be respected

* Calling on a *totem animal* or spirit person who is strong and cares for you to stand and guard your boundaries although this is only a first-aid measure for eventually you want to be able to:

Step up to the plate for yourself, securing your place on this planet with compassion and strength and making it clear to everybody that you are here to stay.

At the end of the day, it may be when the perpetrator crosses into a vital no-go area for the last time that your self-worth eventually snaps and says, *"If this is life, it's not worth existing. There has to be a better way!"*

* * *

DRIVERS OF MANIFESTATION

*Dreams come true when we turn **instinct** into **hoping** to **believing** to **knowing** and then to **being**.*

Have you ever experienced a time when knowing what you were to do in the future came apparently out of the blue but so instantaneously that there was no doubt or need to question. This happened to me shortly after my mother died when, lost in the grieving process, my focus only went as far as how I was going to get from one moment to the next. However, a casual enquiry as to my future brought forth a reply that changed my life, *"So what do you plan to do now, start up a clinic?"*

"No," came my immediate answer, *"I'm going to America,"* and here I am two years later.

I hadn't even considered this as an option in my life and yet some part of me had obviously already made the decision, for as I spoke those words my whole body resonated with the *rightness* of the statement without a moment of hesitation. This state of knowing was not a head-orientated event but a whole-body phenomenon.

As I was told many years ago: *If you are excited by an event in the future, it means it has already happened somewhere on another dimension and is just waiting to be brought into 3D reality...* And I was excited!

Now was the move without fear and trepidation? *No way!*

Did I have my doubts? *You bet!*

But every time those doubts arose I thought about staying where I was and saw all the doors were closed and there was no going back as that part of my life was finished.

Did I know where I was going (apart from America) and what I'd do there?

No, and that was unnerving as I couldn't control the outcome.

But it became clear that the more I let go of control, the more new doors opened and the more I tried to use my small will to determine my future, the more I met brick walls.

* * *

When talking about power we also need to consider the driver or motivator type of fuel, i.e. what emotion and what drives the action. For example, I can wish with passion or with fear and believe with apprehension or with anger. Taking this one step further, it's useful to see the different *fuel drivers* available to us in the creative process and to recognize that, as we move through hoping and thinking to knowing, our success as alchemists increases substantially due to:

* Enhancement of a right relationship as the barriers dissolve between mind/body, spirit/matter and ourselves/the Source

* The willingness to take increased conscious responsibility for our creations

* Reduced attachment to the result

* Less desire to win and more to merge and become unified.

Each psycho-spiritual driver can also be allied to a physical source of fuel which is available on this Earth and reveals which is the most cost efficient (as above so below).

There are five main fuels/forces that are used for most of our creative activities:

1. *Instinctual, physiological, practically unconscious;* little or no connection between the vehicle and its driver, between spirit and matter. Primarily survival-based, aimed at maintaining the body in an optimal state of well-being, similar to the maintenance of a car, without any deeper purpose. The unconscious state is encouraged when shame, fear, despair or apathy are

added to the fuel tank. *(Base chakra.)*
Energy cost: 95 per cent outgoing and five per cent in
return; the pleasure of having a healthy and well-oiled
vehicle.

2. *Emotional mixed with lower psychic activity expressed
   as hoping, wishing, desiring, wanting;* semi-conscious as
   the vehicle and driver start to develop a new
   relationship. This energy is commonly used in power
   games where one person gains at the expense of another
   using large amounts of manipulation and the incitement
   of guilt, duty, anger, control, etc. Always associated with
   large doses of expectation. *(Solar plexus chakra.)*
   Energy cost: 75 per cent output to receive 25 per cent in
   return... Ultimately energy is always lost in power games
   despite an apparent win.

3. *Mind power stimulating the mental body expressed
   through willing, trying, bargaining, believing, or
   thinking;* employing increasing levels of conscious
   intention and a working relationship between mind and
   body. Associated with the use of crystals, color and
   sound. On a negative level, mind power can be used
   against those who act primarily through the first two
   energy sources and energy is lost through stubbornness
   and the tendency to lock horns with a similarly willful
   individual. *(Throat chakra.)*
   Energy cost: 50 per cent output to receive 50 per cent of
   energy in return.

4. *Knowing from the place of the heart (compassion) and
   third eye (detached wisdom), expressed also as allowing,
   merging and flowing;* the strength now comes from
   within and an expanding connection to the Universal
   flow of energy and consciousness. Personality and Soul
   work as one with clarity of perception, an intimate

connection to "right" timing and an optimal use of energy without waste. Associated with symbols, sacred geometry and higher frequencies of light and sound. *(Heart and third eye chakras.)*
Energy cost: 25 per cent output to receive 75 per cent in return.

5. *Being where there is no separation between ourselves and the Source;* there just is! Enlightenment. *(Crown chakra.)* Energy cost: zero per cent output to receive 100 per cent in return.

* * *

When we compare the list above with fuels that are available on this planet this correlation appears:

1. *Instinctual = fossil fuels such as coal, gas and oil.* Taken from dead materials that have little or no life force and hence negligible connection between spirit and matter. Linked with foods that are processed or vitamins and minerals robbed of their connection with the Earth.

2. *Emotional = power from the denser form of the elements such as wind, solar, hydro- and hydrogen-based.* Here the life force is still present providing the basis for a relationship between the world of spirit and matter. Linked also with live foods that are recently taken from the soil especially when organic and where they have been grown with your own fair hands.

3. *Mental = power from breath, prayer, meditation, right thought.* The ability to take in energy through the breath, or the use of the mind to direct energy. Nuclear power is a link between emotional and mental although we are still uncertain how to use this wisely. Associated with

those who live on "air" or generate energy through Tai Chi, Qi Gong or some forms of meditation.

4. *Knowing = exchange of energy between all life forms.* Whether of the Nature Kingdoms, Earth energy lines, other people or the Galaxy, drawing directly on the life force. This exchange is dependent on right relationships and sacred reciprocity where there is a flow of energy without attachment. This is pure alchemy, with the ability to draw energy in through the pores of our being in the name of love or connection.

5. *Being = pure light energy.* Constant supply of pure energy from the Source. No need for external energy as "fed" from within. Unification.

The fuels become less dense and faster as we move from "instinctual to being" emitting less pollution and hence offering greater benefits to the Planet and our own spiritual well-being. The Ancient People would say that our aim is to move individually and as a race from the denser fuels to the lighter ones, reducing the amount of smog that prevents us from connecting on a deeper level.

Chapter Eleven

The Passage of the Serpent

As a true alchemist, we need to gain the skill of working with the elements, fire, water, earth and air, for these are the tools of our trade. They are each as important as the next and yet it is our understanding of fire and how it relates to the passage of the serpent that we will address first.

THE FORCE OF FIRE AND LIGHT

Fire represents spirit with its power to invigorate, enlighten, transform and activate, resulting in the quality of joy. The yang power of fire is its ability to heat, transform and energize thoughts or ideas into manifestation, while the yin quality brings light, *informing* us of our world and encouraging us to seek further. This combination is reflected in the light and warmth of the sun whose very existence we often take for granted. However, one only has see the effect of limited sunlight on large groups of people who suffer the depression of Seasonal Affective Disorder to know how vulnerable we are to the lack of these electromagnetic light rays.

Fire is the motivating spirit that enables the embryo to start to evolve, the fetus to move and the baby to be born. It is the impetus for every activity from the first breath to the last, much of which is unconscious and yet ever-encouraging us to reach our highest potential. It is the feminine Shakti energy which paradoxically holds within it the male Shiva force whose full form will be recognized when the serpent reaches the crown chakra.

Fire is the sleeping serpent or kundalini energy who lies curled at the base of the spine and is activated by acts of creation and exhilaration including during sexual intercourse. For thousands of years, myths have been created around the evil nature of the snake, serpent or dragon energy, ordaining that this force should be subdued at all costs and denying many the power and reconnection that their souls seek. But the time for such travesty of the truth is over and the collective serpent is on the rise and nothing will stop it now.

As the serpent awakens, it is our responsibility as individuals to learn to manage this energy, for like the sun's rays it can be both destructive and as well as bring growth. Hence we have phrases such as, *"I'm all fired up,"* but also, *"I'm burnt out,"* the latter spoken when the serpent is unbridled and allowed to rule the show. Our journey is to master and engage this powerful energy so that we might use it wisely for soul growth and development.

With increasing consciousness comes greater responsibility. Therefore, at every level the challenge is to use this power to instigate creative co-operation, abundance, growth and freedom, all in the name of compassion rather than stimulating greed, coercion, destruction and oppression. The latter appear when the fire of spirit is *cold* and hasn't been warmed by the love and acceptance of the heart and hence there are feelings of disconnection and rejection.

Creating doorways for the serpent

In esoteric terms, there are three nerves that connect the base of the spine to the head, called ida, pingala and sushumna, and it is along the central nerve, the sushumna, that the serpent ascends, passing through each chakra in turn. As it enters the more yang-inspired centers (base, solar plexus and throat) it brings *fire power*, while in the yin centers (root, sacral and heart) it offers its *light* to inform and open the focus of consciousness.

Once the kundalini starts to rise, it is not uncommon for an individual to experience supernatural visions, increased psychic sensitivity, non-local awareness, physical changes and the awakening of creative intelligence. These can be unsettling but merely represent a realignment of energetic pathways to receive this new energy.

The serpent is unable to achieve its mission without *air* offering movement, *earth* bringing strength and *water* holding the intention while the fire acts upon it. The alchemist works constantly with the various elements seeking to bring each center to its maximum potential and hence create doorways or portals through which the serpent will pass on its journey towards the crown chakra, above which Shiva awaits Shakti's arrival.

These portals are very similar to those found within our planet which permit access to the different dimensions above and below the planet's surface, only now we are accessing our own interdimensional status. Here, once again, we are reminded that the body is the universe in miniature and energetically offers the path of initiation so that the soul can attain enlightenment.

The serpent's journey occurs through the following process:

1. We experience each chakra through the **creative cycle**, forming the first loop.

2. We balance this with an understanding and integration of the **duality** at this center.

3. We meet and accept ourselves in all degrees of this duality to its **fullest potential** and hence create a tension between the poles of existence which exposes the door, allowing the serpent to slide through.

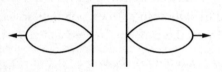

This is fundamental to spiritual alchemy:

The serpent's ascension and hence the opportunity for us to reach our full power and potential is based on our ability to create doorways or portals through which it can pass. These are formed through our willingness to meet ourselves in all poles of existence and to embrace and integrate each part into our being in the name of love. This is true forgiveness. Wherever there is fear, there is a part of us that lacks connection and hence the door will fail to open until reconnection is complete.

Sacred numbers and symbols

In esoteric studies, it is seen that each doorway is represented by a different symbol or vibration, and with its own phrase by which the door will open. However, I was advised by an Elder that, even if we know the words to open the door, it's more important to know the words to exit, otherwise it is easy to become trapped in one dimension and unable to freely move between the worlds.

The five primary *tattvas* or symbols relevant to the Hindu tantric teachings that are connected to alchemical practices and the search for unity, include:

The Base (Muladhara) chakra; a yellow square symbolizing the element earth and called *Prithivi*

The Sacral (Svadisthana) chakra; a silver/white crescent moon lying on its back with the ends pointing upwards associated with the element water and called *Apas*

The Solar Plexus (Manipura) chakra; a red/orange equilateral triangle with its apex pointing upwards associated with the element fire and called *Tejas*

The Throat (Vishuddha) chakra; a blue circle and representing the element air and known as *Vayu*

The Third Eye (Ajna) chakra; an indigo eclipse like the shape of an eye, linked with the element of spirit and called *Akas.*

Practitioners of this study would continuously meditate on each of these shapes merging with the color, element or form until they achieved stability in this area. The result was variable for, as warned above, these symbols are not to be played with as they access ancient memory and, without knowing the way back, the student could easily become lost in fantasy.

In Hindu tradition, five is an important number representing the five bodies of human existence. In contrast, four is afforded great status in the Western world with the four directions, the four gospels, Jung's four functions of the mind and many structures and buildings designed around this number. Four affords us the experience of linear awareness within this Earth, and yet the square, linked to the base chakra, can both be a springboard for our life and our coffin unless we are willing to move up a vibration to the number five.

Here, awareness changes to cycles and spirals as the four directions move around a central point, and hence the four limbs are guided by the head and the thumb engages with each finger generating expansion of light energy through the creative cycle. To the Chinese and Islamic faith, five is highly valued, represented by the *pentagon and five-pointed star* and seen as the number of human existence, with four symbolizing completion on earth and five, moving man into his transpersonal nature. Hence five is connected to health (four) and love (one) for through love's connective nature we are moved to the next level of existence. There are also four elements on this Earth plus a fifth, ether, and five senses: vision, hearing, touch, taste and smell, with the *sixth sense* transforming man into a complete relationship with his soul.

The five-pointed star with its apex pointing upwards, seen in many Egyptian hieroglyphs, represents aspiration towards a point of origin and is linked with education. However, transmuting the symbol and directing the apex downwards has been commonly linked with black magic.

As a point of completion, a six-pointed star, created by two triangles interlinked, is also known as the *Star of Solomon* or the *Star of David*. This is the star on which man can reach his spiritual potential and represents his soul with the marriage between consciousness (the upper triangle or fire) and unconsciousness (the lower triangle or water). Both aspects of consciousness are subject to the immaterial, which is represented by a central point in many cultures. This star is the masculine equivalent of the feminine seed of life which consists of six circles or interlinking vesica piscis (unified duality) around a central circle. When the six pointed star and the seed of life interconnect, we see another sacred marriage occur between the masculine and feminine, symbolizing our ascension to a new level of existence.

The serpent's journey

The journey of the serpent involves its connection to the webs of consciousness above and below our upright form and therefore include two additional chakras to the usual seven: one above the crown where Shiva sits waiting, *the star child*; and the root chakra which is beneath the feet, *the earth child*. All exhibit masculine/feminine aspects as well as qualities of force and focus. However, for simplicity, I am going to concentrate on the main feature which shows itself through each chakra and how we, through our inner work, can open the doorway through which the serpent will eventually pass.

Starting with the root chakra, which represents feminine *focus*, we see a *bow*, *vessel* or *chalice* with its receptive and nurturing qualities as well as its capacity to expel when the appropriate time comes. The next chakra is the base which represents masculine *force* and can be described as the arrow or projection seeking its target all the while willing to sacrifice itself for the goal. As we move up the sushumna, we encounter alternate focus and force with the serpent powered up by the yang-motivated chakras and then diving into the fluid-filled yin vessels, often aided by suction on the part of that center leading to alchemical transformation.

Eventually, force and focus unite at the third eye, expressing the divine state of presence. Now the serpent waits until, through the power of the breath, it is released towards its target: the crown chakra, with its associated pineal gland. This alchemical reaction stimulates, on a physical level, the pineal gland to produce its hormones which, along with its energetic counterpart, leads to expansion of consciousness, ascension beyond the confines of this 3D world and unification with the Source.

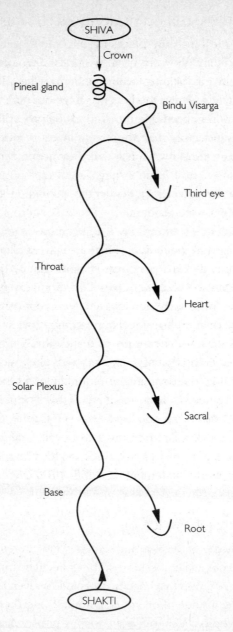

Ascent of the Serpent

The Root Chakra: under the feet (vessel: focus)

One of the most insecure places for our soul's existence is at the root of our being, the very place we first make contact with this planet and its inhabitants, located under our feet. It's no coincidence that we were designed to encourage our "sole" to touch the ground every time we walk. If this "docking procedure" is incomplete or unsatisfactory then feelings of insecurity are inevitable. I meet so many people who feel that they never arrived or never wanted to arrive and, even if they did, always felt an outcast to their culture, family, country, gender etc. No wonder disassociation and addiction is one of the greatest diseases across the world.

Without adequate "rounding" (the feminine of grounding), it is extremely hard to make deep relationships, as friendships must offer a security that is absent from the individual's life and hence tend to be intense experiences based on short-term needs. It's also not uncommon for such individuals to feel more comfortable with the unconditional qualities of Nature, or in prayer and meditation, in a desperate effort to return to an idealized world of spirit, unaware that God is present in everybody they meet.

However, like the magnificent mountains and the tall trees in the forest, we need to root ourselves in this world, for that is the divine vessel that is offering itself to us at this time. By being conscious of our soul/sole upon this Earth every time we walk, and pointing our feet forward in the direction we chose to go, we are making a powerful statement that says: *I BELONG*.

Base Chakra (arrow: force)

This is the home of the sleeping serpent who can remain relatively unconscious in its lair, basking in the collective structure created by the tribe or group that encompasses it. However, like a teenager experiencing a surge of energy that reminds him/her of their own destiny, the base chakra offers a doorway into a whole new world of existence.

It is here that the individual will meet issues of control and security often associated with a range of fears which include:

* Fear of change and the unknown

* Fear of failure and success

* Fear of abandonment, rejection and isolation.

As discussed in an earlier chapter, these fears can feel real but may be an illusion, preventing us from seeing the whole truth. This chakra relates to our willingness to *serve*, not from a place of lack or its associated greed but to walk the path that we choose in honor of the Greater Plan. This sense of service is put to the test when our need to belong, or any of the fears given above, causes us to become *slaves* and not *servants* whether to a belief, emotion, religion or our tribe.

So at this first initiatory doorway of *service*, stability is achieved when we accept and integrate our *controller* and our *slave*, using the appropriate phrase: *I SERVE*.

As the serpent dives into the water of the root, releasing the intention it holds, a sacred marriage occurs, allowing the serpent to pass through the first vesica piscis represented by the vulva.

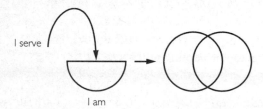

Sacral Chakra (vessel: focus)

As we move to the area just beneath the umbilicus, we encounter the next alchemical vessel which relates to the uterus in women and prostate in men and represents the ability to create right relationships through integration. Symbolically, the physical meeting between the egg (vessel) and sperm (serpent), is a constant reminder of the inner union between poles of existence which lead to new life, not through synthesis but through progression. This chakra is probably one of the most challenged over the centuries in both men and women due to the distorted mythology that surrounds such a perfect experience.

The spiritual quality available in this area is *respect* where every relationship is sacred and hence the name. However, it has often been associated with abuse and shame causing the individual to shrivel inside and the vessel to become closed, with its fluid dark and unwelcoming. Yet, through simple methods, we can start the process of repair and renewal. These include:

* Only allowing into your life those things that nurture your soul

* Appreciating that there have always been those who supported you even in your darkest moments

* Releasing any sense of over-responsibility or martyrdom which often masks a lack of caring for yourself

* Sharing your hidden self in small and safe ways

* Allowing others be the "strong one" without regret or resentment

* Releasing shame and secrets through listening, embracing, accepting and forgiving.

When we are willing to enter this sacred vessel and find a love for the lovable and refuse entry to abuse, we experience a transformation of energy, opening the door to a world of healthy relationships, not just with other people but with all aspects of the Divine. Hence the ability to know *dependence and independence* creates the poles of existence which hold open the door of *interdependence* and a *respect for all life*.

The phrase associated with this is: *I RELATE.*

The Solar Plexus (arrow: force)

As the serpent reaches this center it meets its own element, fire, and feels very much at home. In my mind, I see the diaphragm, above the solar plexus, painted with a sky with a sun and clouds, deluding those who are only attached to their ego's journey, into believing that they have arrived. In truth, the journey is just beginning and they have been fooled by the trickster of illusion and become trapped in their own astral web.

This center demands that we have the courage to reach out and grasp the head of the serpent, our own personal power, focusing its eye of intention so that we might thread it through the eye of the needle, the vesica piscis of the diaphragm. As mentioned previously, this can only occur when we have unburdened ourselves of our attachment to expectations, demands and insecurity. Where there is still poor self-worth and need for approval, despite the façade, this process is made more difficult by the fact that the serpent is often uncontrolled, twirling and spitting at everybody, like a hose of water that has been suddenly turned on without first directing the focus. These individuals demand attention whether through manipulation, unrealistic expectations, anger, victim mentality or threats and it's often easier to stay out of their way until they see that they will be denied what their soul seeks until they tame their own serpent.

Others have such a weak serpent that it hardly makes it to the door, laden as it is with self-doubt, self-deprecation and an unwillingness to secure the hole that continually drains any accumulation of self-worth. Both aspects will only reach mastery when the individual comes to appreciate that their happiness and self-worth is completely in their hands and they cease looking to others for approval or to meet their expectations.

It is only when we are unaffected by criticism or fame that we become masters of our own personal power.

The doorway that awaits the serpent at the solar plexus is held in tension by knowing and accepting the parts of us that can be both *coercive* and *self-deprecating*, allowing the serpent to glide through on the energy of *honoring our own power*.

The appropriate phase is: *I HOLD STRONG.*

As the serpent dives into the waters of the sacral chakra releasing the intention held within, an alchemical reaction occurs and the second vesica piscis is created in the diaphragm and the serpent glides through to the heart.

The Heart Chakra (vessel: focus)

Now the serpent sits within the center which represents our transpersonal self and, like the root, sacral and third eye, is a sacred vessel of transformation. Its mission is dependent on the stability of the sacral and root chakras, for only then can the multi-petalled form open to receive the serpent. Many speak of *opening the heart* as if it were achieved merely through intention. But just as you would not force open the petals of a bud before its time, nor should opening of the heart be forced or rushed.

Fortunately, there is an abundance of stimuli available that can assist in this process such as the sound of a child's laughter, a beautiful sunrise, evocative aromas and the play of dolphins amongst the waves. It is through the arts and senses that fire and water meet in this center with the potential to manifest any idea or inspiration held within the heart's creative vessel. Our role is to steady the waters contained within, mastering the emotions that may wash in from the solar plexus below, and root ourselves into the earth.

If we fail to achieve stillness in the heart then creativity moves from soul manifestation into delusion and madness, often expressed as schizophrenia. In my opinion, one of the vital stages of rooting occurs during the ages of four to five and a half when children play "make believe" within the arena of the physical world. Nowadays, with the advent of computers and less play being out of doors, this connection into the earth is missing and

I believe this is a major factor in the rapid rise in many mental disorders, especially in the young. At the other end of the scale, we meet those who have lost all sense of joy, the water within the vessel turning to ice and their lives driven by fear rather than love. Illnesses such as depression and heart disease represent this joylessness but once again it is through the arts, stimulated by the serpent, that the heart starts to open and the sun pours in.

It is by understanding and appreciating the parts of us that *despair* as well as our *madness* that the door is held in the place of *joy* and the serpent slides through using the phrase: *I EMBRACE*.

Throat Chakra (arrow: force)

So now the serpent sees the end in sight and it faces one of its biggest challenges, for here in the throat, the issue is one of my will versus thy will. The throat seeks to express itself and the serpent can feel its own power. When there is no bowing to a Greater Will, we meet:

* stubbornness

* an endless round of excuses and questions

* control through words

* over-analysis

* fear of letting go and trusting

* constant attempts at bargaining which when unsuccessful can turn to threats

* empty words

* silence

In the end, all the discussion in the world (which the throat chakra revels in) will not result in movement for the serpent, because it is only when we let go to the unknown that the serpent can continue on its way.

The pillars of this door are reflected in the *under and over use of creative expression* and, when these are appreciated in the name of love, the door of *wisdom* opens with the phrase: *I EXPRESS*.

And as the serpent dives into the waters of the heart chakra releasing the intention held within, an alchemical reaction occurs and the third vesica piscis is created between the vocal cords, with the serpent gliding through to the head.

The Crown Chakra

As the serpent moves towards the crown chakra for the first time, it meets an important challenge, for here we face our spiritual pride or arrogance, which can be our ultimate downfall. A metaphor would be like pushing a heavy rock to the top of a mountain, only to stand back in self-importance and see it fall back down into the valley below.

It is at this point we learn humility and the willingness to bend our head, surrendering to a higher power. This is seen in ancient cultures such as the Japanese who build the doorways to their tea-houses specifically low to signify that only those who are willing to bow their heads are allowed to enter. It is also the reason why cultures tend to cover or see as sacred the posterior fontanelle situated towards the back of the head, for this is the area that reaches towards the heavens when our head is bent.

Such surrender is embraced by those who see humility not as a weakness but as a strength of the soul. Imagine the ecstasy experienced by a droplet of water that has traveled hundreds of miles from the icy mountains when it is embraced by the mighty ocean. Our soul yearns for such a connection and willingly surrenders its identity to the Greater collective. It is then that the soul is free of the attachments of the earth and the individual is sovereign of his/her own life, ready to be a leader or guardian of others and be afforded the mark of Cain.

The door at this level is held by our knowledge of the tensions between *arrogance* or *oppression* and *self-defeat* with the union leading to a doorway through which the serpent passes known as *sovereignty* with the phrase: *I LEAD.*

The Third Eye (vessel: focus)

And so the serpent turns its head towards the earth again and enters the third eye which represents our *intention to create*. With the aid of the serpent, the aim of the alchemist is to eventually raise all their energies from below into this one center. This place has the capacity to hold, in perfect balance, the meeting of opposites and to unify them into a common force: the state of presence. It is represented in the physical body by the pituitary gland with its two lobes, one symbolizing spirit and one matter, or the meeting of the masculine and feminine.

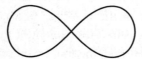

The sign of infinity – the perfect meeting of opposites

Whereas the root was the vessel for the physical world, the sacral chakra a vessel for our human existence, and the heart a vessel for the soul, this center, also known as the ajna, is the vessel of *spirit*. It waits patiently, detached from our lower nature and personal needs for an impulse from our higher self, bringing with it a connection to the Source. Hence this vessel or container represents the powers of discernment, detachment, clarity, patience and thus wisdom. It is the very essence of perfect presence for, like a cat stalking its prey, it can remain entirely still while maintaining a dynamic strength within its structure, ready to act at any moment.

To achieve this state we need to learn to calm our impatience and the tendency to threaten or bargain when things are not happening at the speed or in the way we would have chosen. These energies emerge from the *throat chakra* below causing little problem to the third eye except a superficial feeling of pressure or anxiety which relates to a fear of *missing out* with not enough time to finish our incarnation. Of course the joke is:

There is nowhere to go, no time to fit into and nothing ever really mattered in the first place.

The door is held open by opposing forces of *detachment* versus *the need to connect*, and when we know and appreciate both the serpent moves through the door of *discernment* with the phrase: *I RESPOND.*

And the serpent dives into its own self, swallowing its tale and becoming the Ouroborus, representing the continuity of life as it passes through the fourth vesica piscis of the eyes.

The serpent's head waits poised over the bridge of the nose, carrying the united masculine and feminine qualities of force and focus, fire on water or the marriage between the sun and the moon. The Incas measured the weight of the spine after death, for this symbolized to them the inner work of the soul. Likewise, it is said that you know a true yogi by the flexibility of their spine. The soul's development is measured by the mastery of the serpent as it ascends the sushumna.

With the completion of the passage of the serpent, a long rod is produced with a curve at the top reminiscent of the shepherd's crook. Like Moses, the shepherd of the Israelites who was told to take a serpent and it became his rod of magic, when the serpent finishes its journey, we too possess a magician's rod or wand and achieve the status of alchemist.

The crown and the star child

Now the serpent, Shakti, turns towards Shiva, waiting at the crown chakra and passes through the creative doorway, bindu visarga, the Gateway to the Cosmic Void. As they meet, the ultimate sacred marriage takes place, activating the associated pineal gland through the union of fires and stimulating light-energy release, revealing us as luminescent beings. This is the union the alchemist seeks when base metal turns to gold, our spirit meets with the Divine and we transcend to new levels of existence.

At last, there is understanding behind the phrase:

Be still and know that I am God

BE STILL – allow the focus to be still as a clear, reflecting mirror

AND KNOW – gather the energies into a force of knowing, merging, allowing

THAT I – the original intention, idea, impulse, the static

AM – the reflected manifestation, the dynamic

GOD – the sacred marriage of the static and dynamic leading to unification and hence to know the Divine

Chapter Twelve

The Elements

Everything within this planet is composed of the four elements, Air, Fire, Water and Earth, and they are derived from a fifth element known *as the breath of the invisible* or *the ether* which is the essence that forms the web of consciousness. For the western mind, we need to be able to see these elements as both a physical reality and a state of consciousness with different frequencies and effects. It is through them and their interconnection that we are able to turn spirit into matter and then back to its wave form again.

We have explored fire in detail as it relates to the serpent, and now we will turn our attention to the other elements without which the serpent and its mission are doomed.

AIR

The purpose of air is to maintain our connection to spirit using the power of the breath, the wind as it shapes our world and the transmission of information whether by speech, song or dance.

These qualities are expressed in the following ways:

* Air is like the mind, unseen except by its results. We know wind exists because of the movement of clouds passing across the sky or by the sound of the wind blowing through the leaves of a tree but in essence it is invisible. So it is with the mind.

* Air is not weak because of this disguise as we know the wind's power can uproot mighty trees or whip the ocean into a storm, just by transferring its attention. So it is with the mind.

* Air is also like the mind, moving and disseminating *spirit in form (fire and earth)* or information.

* Air as breath is essential for speech whether involved in the movement of the chest and diaphragm, its passage through the vocal cords, or for modulating the speech in the sinuses.

* Air as vibration is essential for hearing, for all sounds are carried in air. This fact was used by the ancient people who believed that connection to the Great Spirit was maintained by air carrying their songs, stories, chants and even smoke endowed with a prayer or invocation to the Creator.

* Air also ensures a connection to our deeper memories and inner being for we all remember being stirred by a piece of music, a poem, an aroma or a favorite song carried on an airwave.

* Air through the breath and other meditative practices are continually re-enforcing our connection to the spirit realms.

* Air with the fire of passion inspires a performer without which they appear flat and cold. When air and fire move

through their being, they entrain us to reach our
highest inspiration.

* Air guarantees a continual flow of information within the
Nature Kingdoms by transferring seeds from one place to
another, aided by the animals of the air such as insects
and birds.

* Air reconnects us to our Source by assisting us in
releasing old outmoded bonds to people and attitudes
and *"blowing away the cobwebs"*. All the elements are
involved in the grief process but air's only concern is to
return us to spirit. Hence the powerful effect of
"scattering ashes" after a cremation as well as the burning
of letters and mementoes that are no longer part of
our history.

* In oriental medicine, air rules the lungs and
large intestine.

* In astrology, air is associated with the signs of Gemini,
Libra and Aquarius.

WATER

Water is considered the mother of all life, holding us in her womb
until we emerge to experience individualization and returning to
her at the end of our life and hence the transporting of the dead
on water, practiced in many traditions. Death of an idea or dream
occurs many times in our life, dissolving it in water and returning it to the Great Cauldron where it is stirred and blended until
we are ready to give birth again.

Other qualities include:

* Water relates to the soul, to fluidity and with emotions
and feelings.

✳ Water is the container of infinite possibilities waiting to be brought into form. It is the living vessel that acts as a mirror, accurately recording everything that touches its surface and holding it until fire, air and earth bring it into manifestation. During dematerialization, water dissolves the memory so that it can return to the web of consciousness or ether.

✳ Physically, water's unique electrochemical properties associated with its hydrogen bonding, allows it to hold the vibrational memory of any substance in an energetic suspension. This is the principle behind homeopathy where substances added to water are diluted beyond the level where science believes that any chemical will be present. Yet such diluted *potencies* are seen to be highly effective.

✳ Water accurately holds memory as seen in the work by Japanese scientist, Masuro Emoto, who shows the capacity of water to organize not just around minerals but also around the vibration of words and thoughts. He encircled a vial containing water with a piece of paper on which certain words were printed and then froze the water abruptly. Clear, crystalline patterns were produced, appropriate to the written message, with the vibration of the word *love* revealing a beautifully balanced, hexagonal design similar to the exquisite symmetry of the petals of a flower. But when the words, *"You make me sick. I will kill you,"* were absorbed by the water, a distorted and broken crystal was created and within its midst was the figure of a man showing pure aggression. Imagine the effects of such words repeated several times a day on someone's crystalline cellular structure and especially on the delicately balanced immune system. ***Words and thoughts have power; use them wisely.***

* Despite this ability, water is without arrogance or self-importance always willing to fall to the lowest position and adapt to the shape of any container.

* Even through it's formlessness, its power carved out the Grand Canyon one mile deep, and its determination to return to the ocean will push through any conceivable obstruction.

* To the Ancient People, water is seen to represent love as an unconquerable essence both because of its power to connect and because of its nebulous or illusionary quality, reflecting a lack of attachment to the outcome. Love is the force that connects us but in itself does not exist.

* Water represents chaos to those who fear losing control forgetting that we are 70 per cent water, 20 per cent air and the rest is made up of sub-atomic particles. Water, like love, awaits our surrender, for it is our destiny.

* As tears, water washes away anything that maintains separation, especially old ties to the past which deny our reconnection to our deeper self.

* Water as tears of joy occur when we remember our connection and there is only unity.

* In oriental medicine, water rules the kidneys, bladder and ears.

* In astrology, water is associated with the signs of Pisces, Cancer and Scorpio.

EARTH

Earth seeks to stabilize and secure and includes the tallest mountain, a grain of sand and the most exquisite crystal. Whereas water holds in nebulous form, earth holds in structure and shape, acting as a container for all the elements at one time whether fire, air or water. As you will see, many of our problems occur due to inadequate levels of the element earth, preferring to get lost in our passions (fire), thoughts (air) or dreams (water).

Qualities include:

* Earth is linked to the physical body, stability and with sensations.

* Earth acts as the vehicle, initially for the ego and then for the soul, relying on the organs of digestion, absorption and elimination to provide the body with the optimal nutrients for the journey. In the uterus, it is from the mother's selflessness that the embryo receives its nourishment which, in a healthy environment, continues until the child is weaned and able to eat the foods directly from the soil. From this time on, the individual looks to the world outside as its nurturing mother as it continues to strengthen its ego boundaries, creating a strong foundation for the soul's growth.

* Of all the elements earth is the most vulnerable to the human psyche as it is dependent on our relationships, each one influencing the strength or adequacy of our rootedness into this world of matter. If the parents possess weak earth energies and hence poor ego boundaries, they will probably be unlikely to provide the selfless nurturing that the child needs.

* Hence earth is essential for grounding especially in the first two years of life otherwise a child seeks its *oral gratification* in other ways, leading in later life to illnesses such as eating disorders, obesity, hypoglycemia, food allergies and smoking, alcohol and drug addiction. On a psychological level, this causes the individual to be

consistently "hungry", causing greed, unrealistic expectations, a survival mentality and difficulties receiving from anyone.

* Earth strengthens within us as we take command of our own nurturing and secure ourselves by practically seeking ways to achieve that goal.

* Earth is selfless, willing to provide form and structure for our dreams and ideas without needing to be the initiator, allowing its form to dematerialize when the time arrives.

* In oriental medicine, earth rules the stomach and spleen.

* In astrology, earth is associated with the signs of Taurus, Virgo and Capricorn.

FIRE

Fire was discussed as we explored the passage of the serpent but here is a summary of its qualities:

* Fire is linked with spirit, the intuition and the power of expansion and transformation.

* Fire is related to the heart, to joy and passion. However, when passion flares out of control, fire can become destructive to anyone who gets in the way, including its owner.

* Fire esoterically is seen in terms of electrical (force) and magnetic (focus) with their union leading to electromagnetic energy similar to that expressed by the sun.

* When used to seek purity, fire will destroy anything that is false.

∗ In oriental medicine, fire rules the heart and small intestines.

∗ In astrology, fire is associated with the signs of Aries, Leo and Sagittarius.

∗ ∗ ∗

It is through the breath (air) linked to the ether that we carry the inspiration which motivates our energy (fire) to act upon the ocean of unlimited potential (water) and cause it to crystallize into form (earth) creating a story, event or person with whom we can engage. Once we fully experience this part of ourselves (earth) and have gained wisdom the air, fire, and water act upon the earth to release the wisdom, or light energy contained within and return it first to the water so that it can be taken by air into the ether.

The stages of grief clearly express the passage of dematerialization:

1. The numbness starts the release from the past. *Earth*

2. The blame, guilt, worry, *"Maybe I could have done more." Air*

3. The anger, *"Maybe they could have done more!" Fire*

4. The sadness, confusion, depression. *Water*

5. The acceptance, forgiveness. *Ether*

As you see, the elements are deeply interconnected and it is useful to meditate on each of the elements in turn and establish a connection with each until you achieve harmony and equality between them. Often we arrive on the planet with disproportional quantities of each reflecting the elemental balance within our natal astrology chart or past-life experiences.

Which element is your strength and where do you notice a lack?

The elements are constantly interacting with each seeking balance, for otherwise:

Earth (structure) can smother fire (joy) leading to
passive aggression.

Earth (structure) can block water (emotions) leading to
frustration and depression.

Earth (structure) can trap air (thoughts) causing
spiritual depression.

Water (emotions) can flood earth (structure) causing chaos
and lack of security.

Water (emotions) can extinguish fire (joy) leading to
depression and lack of enthusiasm.

Water (emotions) can drown air (thoughts) generating
confusion and disorientation.

Air (thoughts) can cause a fire (passion) to burn out
of control.

Air (thoughts) can whip up water (emotions) into a storm
causing ripples of fear.

Air (thoughts) can lead to a sand (structure) storm creating
chaos and confusion.

Fire (passion) can scorch the earth (structure) causing it
to collapse.

Fire (passion) can evaporate water (emotions) creating mist
and insensitivity.

Fire (passion) can heat air (thoughts) leading to
mental overload.

Yet it also works in reverse, for example:

* Water without fire causes the water to freeze leading
  to impotence.

* Fire without water leads to hot air.

* Earth without fire causes it to be cold and unwelcoming.

* Air without earth lacks containment for thoughts leading
  to regret and delusion.

To the alchemist, balancing the elements is essential to gain perfect mastery of their materials. Initially, it can help to work with the elements in their external form such as:

* Breathing exercises (air)

* Singing, toning and chanting (air)

* Sharing one's truth, prayer, poetry, storytelling (air)

* Burning incense (fire and air)

* Dance and hearing music (air)

* Swimming, lying in a hot tub or in spa water (water and fire)

* Swimming with the dolphins or within the deep ocean (water and air)

* Dissolving into laughter and letting go of constraints (water and fire)

* Getting in touch with a passion (fire)

* Finding something that excites you (fire)

* Lighting candles to bring in new light (fire and air)

* Enjoying a sunrise or sunset (fire and earth)

* Walking without shoes (earth)

* Creating a home that feels secure (earth)

* Using crystals for healing (earth, air and fire)

* Pottery, woodwork, sculpture (earth)

* Gardening, working with animals or the plant kingdom (all the elements)

These techniques were understood by the Ancient People to be essential for the maintenance of a healthy co-operation with the elements, ensuring a flow of creative energy through their own being, their family, land and country.

Chapter Thirteen

Cycles of Change – A Brief Study of Astrology and Numerology

ASTROLOGY

Force + Focus + Stage = Action

The Planets reflect the motivating force or attitude

The Signs reflect the focus or purpose

The Houses relate to the arena or stage

Intention (force + focus) + Perception = Action

I am sometimes asked how can I believe in such an illogical study. In the past, I attempted to supply scientific data in defense of my argument but nowadays my answer is, *"How did you forget?"*

Astrology is the study of nature's cycles and movements with our natal or birth charts, providing us with a map so that we might navigate our journey through life. The chart, a reflection of cyclical awareness, sits at the edge of chaos, between unlimited opportunities and the world of manifestation, expressing a potential waiting to be birthed. The astrology wheel represents the web of energy with all its energy lines into which the soul walks as it commences its incarnation, causing the wheel to start to spin at the initial contact of the soul with its journey.

It is designed so that we might know ourselves from as many angles as possible through stimulating the different forces within us (planets), changing focus regularly (signs) and appearing on a variety of stages (houses). Astrology allows us to activate and experience the holographic universe, expanding the study far outside our present physical existence. Certain patterns are destined to occur, although the actual details are still in the ether and are dependent on our level of consciousness at any particular time. Every planet, sign and house is interconnected, like performers in an orchestra, even though each has a different function and different frequency. Similarly, our chart does not stand alone but, like cogs in a wheel, it is intricately linked to all those we meet on our journey and with those within the spirit world who are so in harmony with our vibration.

Like every part of this journey, astrology is about relationships and the impact on our soul when we engage with such powerful forces. It is my intention to provide a simple introduction to astrology to hopefully whet your appetite to take the study further. So we begin with:

The planets

There will be specific times in our life when we will be presented with our soul's blueprint and asked:

"Are you fulfilling your chosen potential?"

At that moment, all our cunning disguises and delusions are exposed for what they are and we come face to face with the truth of our existence. The examiner is the planet *Saturn* who faithfully carries the plan we designed before entering this earth plane and every approximately 28 years brings it out for re-inspection. Hence, between the ages of 27–29, 55–57 and again between 83–85, we are asked the question:

"So where are you going and is this it?"

Saturn is strong on accountability especially since his other name is *Cronus*, the ruler of time, and few escape his keen eye watching to see if you are complying with the *to do list* that you designed prior to incarnation. Some people receive gentle nudges of remembering every seven years (4 x 7 = 28) and hence the concept of the seven-year itch. At these times, we review our lives and, because Saturn is also linked with structure, we may find ourselves settling into a new job, moving home or starting a family. However, more commonly, Saturn's desire for form feels like restriction and we start to see areas in our life where we feel trapped and not living the life we chose. At this point many people break free of beliefs, partnerships or jobs that are limiting, striving to recall their deeper calling and carve their path synonymous with that impulse.

I was 28, engaged to be married, about to start a career as a general practitioner and adapt to a conventional way of life when a small, persistent voice arose from within, urging me to hear:

"There's more to life; don't settle for less. Trust everything will work out."

This was before I had any idea about astrology or the movements of planets, and I really thought I was going crazy especially as I was surrounded by college mates who appeared perfectly content with their future lives. However, the voice would not go away and eventually, following a year's work experience in New Zealand, I emerged with a totally new view on life, opening myself to all the psychic and esoteric knowledge that had been part of my childhood, and I've never looked back.

Saturn rules Capricorn, the sign of the mountain goat, which shows its strength by being duty-bound, responsible and determined. Capricorns love a challenge, making lists of lists and forever sorting their life into orderly boxes. One story of Capricorn is that when everybody reaches the top of a mountain after a long, hard climb and are admiring the view, Capricorn said, *"Look, there's another mountain to climb!"*

Anyone who has strong Capricorn energy has to learn to take the easier path which is a challenge in itself for such responsible individuals. This same determination is seen in Saturn, its ruler, who is also seen as the teacher. It is said that wherever Saturn sits in your natal astrology chart will show you what you are here to learn. However, such lessons are not a judgment but rather Saturn revealing where petals are still held closed, where our challenges will appear and the probable source of our greatest achievements.

If we use this to explore how astrology unfolds, we see that someone who chooses *Saturn in Capricorn*, will often find themselves born into a family where duty and responsibility are important or where cultural rules define the behavior of the individual. Such structure offers a secure sense of belonging but may also inhibit freedom of action. The path of this soul is to learn to take responsibility for their own decisions, defining their own rules of behavior and acting from inner guidance rather than from external rules.

Since Saturn is also the teacher, I often find that if we teach what Saturn is attempting to teach us, we free ourselves of its restrictive nature. Hence with this placement we see teachers of accountancy (facts and figures), personal trainers (physical form) and teachers of chiropractic or osteopathic techniques (since Capricorn rules our bones).

On the other hand *Saturn in Pisces* would reveal a household where dreams, fantasy and creativity were frowned upon and the journey of this soul would be to find a way of structuring their creativity through professions that include film-producing, exhibitors of art, and sculptors. If an outlet for their creative mind was not found they could easily become depressed, resentful and withdrawn.

This simple explanation of Saturn's influence on our life reflects what all Ancient People knew, which was that the planets have a powerful influence on our relatively delicate systems just as a full moon will affect the tides. Each planet is seen as a mythological archetype with its own particular qualities and energetic frequencies that represent our own psychological drives and urges. In other words, each planet brings a different color and level of brightness to the pure white light, transforming kundalini energy into an attitude or motivational force.

For instance:

* *The sun* shines forth, expressing the rhythm of our personal life and what we seek to reveal as an individual. It sits at the core of our being and reflects our father's line or dynasty.

* *The moon* reflects and reveals an energy related to past endeavors, how we will react when we feel stressed and to the energy received from our mother or bloodline.

* *Mercury* explores and communicates.

* *Venus* harmonizes and loves.

* *Mars* asserts and masters.

* *Jupiter* expands and enlivens.

* *Saturn* holds and instructs.

* *Uranus* rebels and invents.

* *Neptune* dissolves and merges.

* *Pluto* destroys and transforms.

* *The Ascendant or rising sign* reveals our soul's purpose, the offering we will make to the world and the energy we'll use to achieve these goals. Its polar opposite, the descendant, shows us where we will meet ourselves in others as it sits at the beginning of the seventh house, the house of relationships. Both need to be understood and accepted if we are to fulfill this incarnation.

The signs

If the planets are the motivating force then the astrological signs are the focus and reveal how the force will manifest. In our natal or birth chart, the planets are found in the signs they were seen in the sky at the time of our birth. If you've never stood and looked out into a clear, night sky and viewed the various constellations you've missed a treat, for only then can you start to understand why the indigenous people trusted the stars to tell them when to begin a whole new cycle.

There are 12 signs, each with its own focus of action and each ruled by one of the planets which gives you a flavor of its energy and intensifies the action when a planet is in its own sign as with the example given above of Saturn in its own house of Capricorn.

Each sign relates to one of the four elements (fire, earth, air, water) and is either *cardinal* (growing), *fixed* (steady) or *mutable* (changeable). Obviously we experience greater stability in our lives if we have a healthy balance of all four elements and modalities but it may not offer so much fun!

Every sign has a polar opposite that will often reveal itself as a shadow sub-personality requiring integration. Both the sign and its dual aspect relate to different areas of the body and, again, both need to be taken into account in the search for well-being. Before looking at the signs in turn, I want to stress that knowing your sun sign is only the start of this fascinating study. Each planet and its sign offer a myriad of information especially when we start to compare how planets relate to each other in the natal chart, what happens when planets are transiting, and the effects of progressed planets through the years. If I stimulate an interest in this subject, I strongly advise you to go and have your natal chart drawn up, plus the transits and progressions, by a qualified astrologer who seeks the widest view of your soul's journey.

As a starting point I offer a few suggestions of areas to focus upon through the signs:

Aries (ruled by Mars, a fire and cardinal sign) seeks self-assertion, initiative and leadership qualities. Aries, the ram, is associated with passion, physical well-being and courage, and enjoys starting projects although completion can be a problem as new ventures easily lead to distraction. Quickly fired up and eager to move, Aries can show intolerance for others or burn out when passion overrides reason. *Aries rules the brain and the head. Libra is its opposite sign.*

Taurus (ruled by Venus, an earth and fixed sign) focuses on security, values, possessions and sensual pleasures, including food, sexuality and touch. Taurus, the bull, seeks the expression of its many gifts and talents but due to a possessive and stubborn nature, there can be a tendency to hoard these, denying the individual their own just deserves. *Taurus rules the throat, neck and thyroid and its opposite sign is Scorpio.*

Gemini (ruled by Mercury, an air and mutable sign) takes our attention to communication, mental activity, problem-solving and analysis. Gemini, the twins, uses its charisma and adaptability to change into whatever is required to initiate communication. Hence, the tendency to be seen as "two-faced" or as a butterfly that lacks commitment. *Gemini rules the lungs, arms and shoulders and its opposite sign is Sagittarius.*

Cancer (ruled by the Moon, a water and cardinal sign) focuses on home, the family and emotions. Cancer, the crab, looks to find harmony and connection whether at home, amongst friends or at work, and offers that to those it meets. Such a desire, however, can cause the formation of "blind spots", for the crab quickly disappears inside its shell at the mere hint of conflict, refusing to admit there is a problem. In the same way, its many legs allow it to sidestep anything that seeks to disturb its comfort zone. *Cancer rules the stomach and breasts and its opposite sign is Capricorn.*

Leo (ruled by the Sun, a fire and fixed sign) seeks to find spontaneity, a joyful heart, the playful child, innocence and creativity. Leo, the lion, wants to shine, to know fame, to be in the limelight, to experience self-confidence and to express itself through its roar. So focused is it on its aims that it can be naïve to the actions of others, show its anger when it's not the center of attention and become reliant on the approval of others. *Leo rules the heart and spine and its opposite sign is Aquarius.*

Virgo (ruled at present by Mercury, an earth and mutable sign) focuses on its quest for beauty, perfection, discernment and the ability to know and enjoy the fruits of its endeavors. Virgo, the virgin, works steadily and carefully towards its goals always seeking the most aesthetic outcome. However, when self-worth is poor, Virgo can become critical both of itself and others, fearful of taking risks for fear of humiliation and with the greatest difficulty of acknowledging its errors. *Virgo rules the intestines and the nervous system and its opposite sign is Pisces.*

Libra (ruled at present by Venus, an air and cardinal sign) pays attention to balance, diplomacy, relationships, integrity, fairness and intellectual pursuits. Libra, the balance, expresses a humanitarian flare, using its mind to observe the larger picture and to treat everyone with honor. The downside of this is that Libra can have extreme problems in making any decision, always wanting the result to be fair for everyone and rarely able to make it fair for themselves. This leads to a tendency to pick over tiny details while denying the larger issues. *Libra rules the kidneys and one level of skin and its opposite sign is Aries.*

Scorpio (ruled by Pluto, a water and fixed sign) seeks depth and transformation in all areas of its existence. Scorpio, the scorpion, is loyal with a strong inner power, a love for the occult, intense feelings, a willingness to stay in a situation until transformation occurs and an ability for silence when the need arises. Scorpio's decision to stay the course can cause hurt and disappointment if others are less committed, leading either to an attempt to strike back or, more often, a case of self-stinging. *Scorpio rules the sexual organs and its opposite sign is Taurus.*

Sagittarius (ruled by Jupiter, a fire and mutable sign) focuses on the search for truth, higher beliefs and philosophy and a spiritual lifestyle. Sagittarius, the archer, lives with enthusiasm, hope and a desire for justice. Its natural confidence, quick-thinking and expansive nature attracts many although there can be a tendency for over-responsibility, impulsiveness and tactlessness. When the archer's fire is stunted by the fears of others, depression can be the result. *Sagittarius rules the hips, thighs and liver and its opposite sign is Gemini.*

Capricorn (ruled by Saturn, an earth and cardinal sign) seeks to experience security through steady perseverance, planning and organization. Capricorn, the mountain goat, is responsible, loyal and practical and can be relied upon to get the job done. But, as already mentioned, the goat can become obsessed by its goals and unable to enjoy the journey. It can also attempt to apply its own need for structure on others causing resentment and isolation. *Capricorn rules the knees, bones, teeth and a level of skin and its opposite sign is Cancer.*

Aquarius (ruled by Uranus, an air and fixed sign) pays attention to the community, the collective, reforms and self-consciousness.

Aquarius, the water carrier, seeks to be unique using its intelligence and self-confidence to achieve this goal and willing to walk alone rather than with those whose philosophies do not resonate with its truth. Such clarity of thought and emotional detachment can run into problems when Aquarian ideas cannot be grounded in reality because of the inability to connect intimately. Physical illness often manifests to encourage an individual to commit to the connection. *Aquarius rules the ankles and circulation and its opposite sign is Leo.*

Pisces (ruled by Neptune, a water and mutable sign) focuses on creativity, imagination, sensitivity, caring and its psychic abilities. Pisces, the fish, works through its intuition to "go with the flow" dissolving barriers that prevent it seeking reconnection to the Source. This lack of boundaries can lead to an impractical nature, hypersensitivity, irrational fears and loss of connection with reality. Grounding is essential if creativity is to be seen. *Pisces rules the feet and immune system and its opposite sign is Virgo.*

* * *

Now if we look at a few examples we see:

* *If Mars is in Gemini* communication will be assertive and even sometimes aggressive.
  When Venus is in Gemini there will be a love of communication or harmony through communication.

* *If Jupiter is in Taurus* expansion will occur in the area of food (weight gain), money (joy of spending) and expression of one's talents.
  When Jupiter is in Scorpio then truth and expansion will occur through the occult, the deep subconscious or intense experiences.

The houses

It is through the houses that we are allowed to see where the "drama" will be played out: the houses are the stage. Hence we see the following correlations:

1st House: our birth, the development of the self

2nd House: money, values, possessions, talents and resources

3rd House: the concrete mind, early education, speech, siblings and short journeys

4th House: home of origin, our inner world, father/mother

5th House: children, play, fun, creative expression, hobbies, romance and sports

6th House: health, service, work, body–mind connection and animals

7th House: point of self-awareness, relationships and our shadow seeking integration

8th House: sex, death and regeneration

9th House: the higher mind, higher education, spiritual philosophies, long journeys

10th House: career, mother/father, ambition and where we desire recognition

11th House: collective, unified field, social consciousness, friendships and utopia

12th House: the unconscious, hidden weaknesses, past lives and addictions

And so:

Mercury in the 5th will allow the individual to express their creativity through the use of their mind such as in poetry, writing or designing. Their children will be brought up with mental pursuits and sports that involve strategy and teamwork.

Uranus in the 5th will see an individual whose creativity has to be unique, otherwise they become bored. They enjoy unusual hobbies and even an unusual love life!

Pluto in the 5th could reveal an individual who is obsessed with finding approval (Leo rules the house) and acts like a child when they are not heard. Creativity and romance involve deep feelings and transformation.

* * *

The seven-year cycle of development

Having discussed Saturn in some depth previously, I believe it is appropriate to explore its relationship to our development, as every seven years Saturn creates a new cycle and we move to a new octave of consciousness. Hence:
0–7 years = development of the consciousness of the physical body
7–14 years = development of the consciousness of the emotional body
14–21 years = development of the consciousness of the mental body
21–28 years = development of the consciousness of the soul body.

The cycle repeats itself so that from 28–56, we seek to fulfill our cycle of maturity, between 56–84 we move into the phase of the elder, and after 84 we start the cycle all over again some living as an ancient one and some reverting back to childhood!

If we then look at specific ages within these cycles, we see that between the ages of 35–42 and 63–70, we will once again be refining our emotional body (second phase of the 28-year cycle). Now each seven years can be further divided into five phases related to oriental medicine's five-element theory. These phases are essential for our ability to live as creative beings and repeat themselves, moving us to a new octave every seven years. Hence:

The first nine months in the womb until nine months after birth. Linked with *kidney energy*, the integration of the ancestral life force and with complete dependency on the parents. This can be a wonderful time of nurturing and learning to receive, or can leave the individual with insecurity and fears when the basic needs go unmet. This energy, linked with the *water* element, is connected to bone and teeth formation and the function of the kidneys and ears. When this phase reappears, we face issues concerned with our security and seek ways to assure that which paradoxically may mean overcoming fears and asking for help.

Nine months – two-and-a-half years
This phase is connected to *liver energy* and the element of *wood*, concerned with decision-making and movement. During this phase a child learns to stand and walk, expanding its range of choices and the speed it can reach them. In a healthy situation, the child is encouraged and given freedom to explore within the boundaries of natural parental care. However, when the child is restricted either physically or in their ability to make decisions due to criticism or control, then the liver energy takes the strain.

In most cases, parents are merely protecting their offspring in the name of love but at some point the child needs to fall and make their own "mistakes", for that will be the only way they will grow. Wood energy rules the liver, gall bladder and eyes as well as the ability to express anger appropriately.

Two-and-a-half – four years
Now the *heart energy* is being activated and the heart forms into a creative vessel associated with communication, connection and the element of *fire*. Here the child extends its exploration using its voice to form deeper connections with the world. It is a wonderful time of chatter, questions, creativity and the development of new friendships. In oriental medicine, the heart meridian links to the base of the tongue and hence if we fail to speak, our heart dies.

You can imagine a home where conversation is not met with love and encouragement especially where there is depression, passive aggression, criticism or secretive behavior. Here a child learns to hold their tongue and keep their own counsel and reaches inside for friendship often resorting to the world of fantasy rather than risking further rejection.

Hence we see the suppression of the fire's natural enthusiasm and joy and in time we may see illnesses related to this involving primarily the heart and small intestine which includes allergies.

Four – five-and-a-half years
At this point, the child's *stomach and spleen energies* are activated, linked to the element *earth*. During this period of a child's life, they are ready to leave the security of their mother's nest and find ways to root themselves as individuals into this earth. Hence, it is often the time when the child goes to school and forms attachments to their teachers and begins the loosening of parental bonds. It is also a time when the child's creativity and imagination blossoms and all manner of make-believe is enacted within their environment whether using furniture, clothes or the outdoors.

This is a vitally important phase, for the child's capacity to embed themselves into the 3D world will ensure their ability to fulfill their soul's purpose. However, if these attachments are not created, stomach energy is poorly generated and the individual will substitute food for roots and creative ideas will remain as a fantasy or dream, with the possibility of the onset of schizophrenia. There is also a tendency to ruminate over everything leading to indigestion from sheer over-analysis and worry. Other illnesses relevant to this area include those of the stomach, spleen and pancreas.

Five-and-a-half – seven years
Finally, we enter the phase ruled by *metal* or *air* and linked to the *lungs*. The child is now ready to step out into the world and learn to fly, aided by secure parents who encourage such independence and who can offer a dependable base for return at any time. However, if a child feels this base is not available, or if they are responsible for the happiness within the family, or their wings are tied due to tribal laws and duty, then problems often occur within the lungs or within the associated large intestine.

The final nine months of this phase starts to reflect the new cycle as the seed grows within the waters of our own soul's womb.

* * *

As we reach each of these phases in our life, the same issues will arise to show us where we are proficient and where work still needs to be done to ensure a smooth, flowing cycle. Hence, someone aged 62 would be meeting their metal energy again and exploring the power of release and their ability to fly while, at age 45, the individual is connecting to their heart and finding ways to communicate clearly from that place.

Summary

These are just a few of the many factors whose energetic frequencies influence our choices from moment to moment ranging from the merely physical to the esoteric. Apart from these, an astrologer will look at the South and North nodes of your moon to appreciate the karmic journey in this life, the position of *Chiron*, an asteroid who represents where you will seek healing, the phase of the moon under which you were born, and the position of many other asteroids and moons which in their own small way will reveal an aspect of the Self.

Astrology is more than knowing your sun sign, it is a profound art, seeking to guide but not to direct. There are no bad planets or signs, just as no color is bad or good, just different. Our charts show us the choices we made before we incarnated, where we will need to focus attention, the energy available to us and where we can look for pleasure, success and enlightenment. As we direct our attention, gather our force and work through our perceptions, we slowly but surely deeply affect the web of consciousness as cycles turn on cycles which turn on cycles.

NUMEROLOGY

This is another important art, valued within most ancient cultures as a means to explore the path the soul has chosen. We owe much of our understanding to Pythagoras, the father of mathematics, who was born in 582 BC in Greece. He saw that the numbers 1 to 9 symbolize universal principles that are played out here on earth, especially through our personal actions. Pythagoras taught that everything was subject to predictable progressive cycles and that:

Evolution is the law of Life, Number the law of the Universe, and Unity is the law of God.

In the beginning was 0, the vacuum, out of which emerges:

1 = the male principle

2 = the feminine principle

3 = the trinity and the manifestation of self-expression

4 = stability, law and order

5 = freedom, expansion to the next level

6 = consciousness and harmony

7 = the search for answers in stillness

8 = power and responsibility

9 = selfless service

There are three other numbers that are considered sacred numbers and that are included in most assessments. These are:

11 = pioneering spirit

22 = inspiration

33 = guardianship

Based on these principles, there are four main numbers that allow us to see our path more clearly:

The Action number: calculated from the addition of the numbers within our birth date, represents the energy that will underlie all our actions.

The Soul number: calculated from the addition of the numbers related to the vowels of our birth name, represents the inner self or urges of the soul.

The Personality number: calculated from the addition of the numbers related to the consonants of our birth name, symbolizes our outer persona and how we will appear to others.

The Destiny number: calculated from the addition of the numbers related to the vowels and consonants of our birth name, signifies what we choose to manifest and achieve in this life.

Obviously, our date of birth doesn't change through life although this is not true of our name, especially where women take on the name of their husband. It is interesting to calculate the soul, personality and destiny numbers based on nicknames, abbreviations and any changes that may have occurred through life, allowing you to appreciate how your frequency alters when you call yourself by a different name.

How to calculate the action number/life lesson number

Add together all the numbers of the birth number, with zero as nil and reduce to a single digit.

For example: 10. 11. 1933 = 19 = 1

This individual's *action number is 1*, symbolizing leadership qualities.

This same result can be achieved by adding the day and month numbers together until a single digit is reached and doing the same with the year of birth and then adding these together to create another single digit. This allows us to see the regular appearances of certain numbers:

$$1\,0.\quad 1\,1.\qquad\qquad 1\,9\,3\,3$$

$$(1 + 0 + 1 + 1)\qquad (1 + 9 + 3 + 3)$$

$$= 3\qquad\qquad\qquad = 16$$

$$(1 + 6)$$

$$= 3\qquad\qquad\qquad = 7$$

$$(3 + 7)$$

$$= 10$$

$$(1 + 0)$$

$$= 1$$

1 = action number

Hence:

3 appears 4 times, hence strong creative energy

1 appears 7 times, leadership qualities intensifying the action number

How to calculate the soul, personality and destiny numbers

1	2	3	4	5	6	7	8	9
A	B	C	D	E	F	G	H	I
J	K	L	M	N	O	P	Q	R
S	T	U	V	W	X	Y	Z	

Y is considered a vowel when it is the only vowel in the syllable e.g. *Cyril* or when it sounds like ee, e.g. *Mary*

W is a vowel when it follows a G or D, e.g. *Gwen*

Example:

M A R Y   J A N E   D A W E S

Vowels: 1   7   1   5   1   5

By addition = 20 = 2 = Soul Number

Consonants: 4   9   1   5   4   5   1

By addition = 29 = 11 = 2 = Personality Number

Vowels + Consonants = 2 + 2 = 4 = Destiny Number

The *inner soul* of Mary Jane resonates with the vibration of 2 which shows her sensitivity and caring. Interestingly, her *outer personality* is 11 (a sacred number) which then breaks down to 2. This allows her an easier path, for her inner and outer worlds are congruent although she will have to watch that her caring nature doesn't cause her to have loose boundaries and become co-dependent. The number 11 means that she will be a pioneer probably involved in the field of care especially as her *destiny number* is 4. This solid number shows that her goal will be to create a stable structure through which her caring and sensitivity can be expressed.

Explanations

The explanations given below summarize aspects of each number that can be applied to both the name and the birth date. For a more detailed exploration, I suggest consultation of the many excellent books now available on the subject.

1 = leader, dominant, willing to go alone, strong, independent, determined, physically active and creative.
   Downside: arrogant, lonely, dictatorial, stubborn. If not in a leadership position will get frustrated with others

2 = caretaker, giving, receptive, selfless, gregarious, loving and warm
  Downside: poor boundaries, poor self-worth, dependent, pleaser, cautious

3 = creative, thinker, architect, needs freedom and looks for beauty, luxury and pleasure
  Downside: Jack-of-all-trades, analyzes everything, fearful of manifesting ideas

4 = builds solid foundation, well-ordered, administrative, responsible and strong
  Downside: can become trapped by the demands of others or their own fears

5 = freedom, enthusiasm, new experiences, communicative, reader and enjoys the public eye
  Downside: butterfly-like, superficial, lacks commitment

6 = responsible to the family, brings comfort to others, seeks harmony, gregarious
  Downside: lacks spiritual depth, no time for self

7 = developed mind, mystic, likes time alone for meditation, strongly intuitive and wise
  Downside: detached, drifts away, difficulty bringing ideas down to earth

8 = powerful, ambitious, administrative, leads by example and enjoys sports
  Downside: power-driven, controller, difficulty having fun

9 = universal lover of humanity, patient, kind and understanding
  Downside: must not seek own ego needs otherwise universal energy fails to flow

11 = altruism, community, strong intuition, high standards, pioneer, scientist

Downside: power may go to the head, impatient, lonely, feels everything intensely

22 = inspirational visionary, sees larger picture and willing to bring it into being
Downside: can be seen as destructive, needs efficiency and courage

33 = strong desire to protect others, loves nature, arts and harmony
Downside: needs to be willing to sacrifice self for the bigger picture

Finally, we can look at the day your were born as follows:

Born on 1st: Leadership skills, willing to take an idea and run with it
Watch: Can become dominating or overbearing

Born on 2nd: Co-operative and efficient in any partnership
Watch: the goodwill can be abused

Born on 3rd: Gregarious, expressive, creative and curious
Watch: important to focus and ground ideas in reality

Born on 4th: Hard-working, strong, capable and practical
Watch: Can be intolerant of those who act in a different way

Born on 5th: Changeable, loves travel, movement, arts and humor
Watch: important to steady the energies and enjoy the ride

Born on 6th: Home-loving, seeks harmony and peace within the family
Watch: be careful not to lose self in the desire to maintain harmony at any cost

Born on 7th: Studious, the mystic whose emotions run deep, needs quiet and solitude
Watch: be careful not to detach from the warmth of relationships

Born on 8th: Powerful, strong, good with finances, responsible and reliable
   Watch: important to give and receive both to yourself and others
Born on 9th: Humanitarian, loves travel, philosophy and esoteric matters
   Watch: observe the needs of the little ego so goodness can flow
Born on 10th: Strong, no problem too great, highly respected for leadership skills
   Watch: be careful not to walk over others
Born on 11th: Idealistic, sensitive, intuitive, protector and brings ideas to reality
   Watch: important not to become over-protective or over-sensitive
Born on 12th: charming, beautiful, loving and intelligent
   Watch: use the charm wisely
Born on 13th: hard-worker, careful planner and devoted
   Watch: make time for play and don't letting planning become procrastination
Born on 14th: intelligent, creative, communicative and enjoys variety
   Watch: important not to let spontaneity lead to foolhardiness
Born on 15th: kind, compassionate, cares for family, seeks justice
   Watch: be careful not to get lost in the problems of others
Born on 16th: Curious, seeks inspiration and knowledge with a quiet charm
   Watch: can become over-analytical especially of self
Born on 17th: Creatively intelligent, vital, whose strength leads to manifestation
   Watch: needs solitude from time to time to recharge batteries

Born on 18th: Double of the 9 and therefore does everything well and successfully

Watch: be patient of others who are less skilled

Born on 19th: Capable and loves adventure and new experiences

Watch: important to master emotions

Born on 20th: Compassionate, great listener, self-sacrificing and loyal

Watch: can become lost in the worlds of others

Born on 21st: bright, sociable, communicative and with a love of people

Watch: careful not to become a social butterfly

Born on 22nd: strong, tenacious, hard-working and can succeed at most things

Watch: important to learn to lay aside personal success to help others succeed

Born on 23rd: changeable, communicative, expressive and affectionate

Watch: will not cope with being tied down

Born on 24th: Dedicated, hard-working, caring for the family and enjoys beauty

Watch: needs to remember to play and have fun

Born on 25th: Patient, trustworthy, wise, considers everything carefully

Watch: can become lost in thought

Born on 26th: Strong, ambitious, intelligent and will probably achieve fame and fortune

Watch: important to balance the love of others with one's own needs

Born on 27th: Versatile with a quick mind, loves the occult and travel

Watch: can get lost in contemplation

Born on 28th: Leader, creative, organized and co-operative

Watch: important to make time for intimacy

Born on 29th: Loves large groups especially where the mind is stimulated

Watch: can get lost in their own self-importance

Born on 30th: Expresses self with charm and abundant talent

Watch: be careful not to allow creativity to be limited

Born on 31st: intuitive, tidy, orderly and with an eye for practical details

Watch: be careful not to get lost in details and forget the self

* * *

It is my belief that these ancient but reliable forms of assessment, which include numerology and astrology, can no longer be excluded from any physical, psychological or spiritual practice without seriously compromising the care of the individual. It would be similar to only hearing one out 10 words spoken or trying to appreciate a tree from a single leaf.

The purpose of these arts is to offer guidance rather than to limit, and to allow any practitioner to truly know their client. But more importantly, these arts allow us to know ourselves, for remember there is no separation between us except in our minds and the vibration of one person always exists somewhere within our own consciousness.

* * *

Our Extraterrestrial Nature

I have left this aspect of the remembering to last, as it is probably one of the least integrated aspects of the self, with many preferring to speak of themselves as angels rather than as ETs (extraterrestrials). However, this is the time to recall that we are all extraterrestrials, originally alien to this planet, arriving from a variety of different "locations" whether within this galaxy or beyond what we perceive as the universe. Some have a deeper knowledge of this truth, having never lost their connection to the other dimensions and many are just waking up. In the near future, there will be increasing evidence of those from different realms visiting this planet to help us in the Great Shift. Let me assure you, many are already here and living amongst us now, including a large proportion of those reading this book. We are experiencing *extraterrestrial encounters* all the time, the problem is that they don't always fit the stereotype.

I believe it's important to stress that those who come to help are advanced souls and hence *shape shift* to take on an acceptable form, with the hope of minimizing fear and anxiety. These beings come in the name of love, wishing to know and aid us and not to take over the world, for these highly evolved groups could have done that at any time with a blink of an eyelid. There has been a huge cover-up of the degree of contact and integration that has already occurred, by those who would choose to suggest that this is for our protection. The true reason is that if we re-establish contact with our universal family and remember who we are, we would no longer be subservient to those who attempt to limit us.

There are many groups who are traveling through space to observe us at this time, just as families and friends come to welcome the new baby. Others come to teach and to share their wisdom although this is easier to achieve when we are in sleep state and we travel from our physical world.

My advice is to listen to any news with the heart of compassion and the eye of wisdom and remember this is the time for reconnection and hence there are a multitude of beings who await your return to the fold with their arms outstretched to reach you.

* * *

So, in summary, our awareness is awakening to a new holographic vision of the universe as our soul reconnects to the web of Christ Consciousness or unity. It asks that we direct our force and focus on only those things that bring joy, health and peace for all inhabitants of this planet whether within, upon or above. It asks that we remember our origins whether these are physical, spiritual or connected to universal energy lines. And most of all, it asks that we enjoy the gifts that are available to all and that can never be denied: the gifts of inner peace, laughter and of love.

Be still and know that I am God.

Bibliography

Shamanism

Michael Harner: *The Way of the Shaman*
Jamie Sams: *Dancing the Dream: The Seven Sacred Paths of Transformation; Other Council Fires Were Here Before Ours; Medicine Cards: The Discovery of Power Through the Ways of Others; Sacred Path Cards: The Discovery of Self Through Native Teachings*
Olga Khariditi: *Entering the Circle*
Mary Sparrow Dancer: *Love Song of the Universe*
Ted Andrews: *Animal-Speak*
Kenneth Meadows: *Earth Medicine*
Serje King: *Kahuna Medicine*
Angeles Arrien: *The Four-Fold Way*
Hank Wesselman: *Spirit Walker; Medicinemaker*
Mary Summer Rain: *Spirit Song*
Marie-Lu Lorler: *Shamanic Healing and the Medicine Wheel*

Regression

Raymond Moody: *Life between Life* (with Brian Weiss); *Reunions*
Michael Newton: *Journey of Souls; Destiny of the Soul*
Brian Weiss: *Many Lives, Many Masters*
Carol Bowman: *Children's Past Lives*
Trutz Hardo: *Children who have Lived Before*

Inspirational

Eckhart Tolle: *The Power of Now*
Zecharia Sitchin: *When Time Began; The 12th Planet, Genesis Revisited, The Lost Realms and Others*
Paulo Coelho: *The Alchemist*
Hal Stone and Sidra Winkelman: *Embracing Our Selves: Voice Dialogue*
Dalai Lama: *The Art of Happiness; Ancient Wisdom, Modern World*
Anthony de Mello: *The Heart of the Enlightened*
Miguel Ruiz: *The Four Agreements*
Adriana Rocha: *A Child of Eternity*
Paramahansa Yogananda: *Autobiography of a Yogi*
Lao-Tzu: *Tao Te Ching*
Viktor E. Frankl: *Man's Search for Meaning*
Andre Van Lysebeth: *Tantra, the Cult of the Feminine*
Francis King: *Tantra, the Way of Action*

Earth Energies and Sacred Geometry

Drunvalo Melchizedek: *The Ancient Secret of the Flower of Life (2 volumes)*
Laurence Gardner: *Bloodline of the Holy Grail; Genesis of the Grail Kings; Realm of the Ring Lords*
Paul Broadhurst and Hamish Miller: *The Dance of the Dragon*
Paul Devereux: *Symbolic Landscapes; Shamanism and the Mystery Lines; Stone-Age Soundtracks*
Chris Morton and Ceri Louise Thomas: *The Mystery of the Crystal Skulls*
Rand Flem-Ath and Colin Wilson: *The Atlantis Blueprint*

Consciousness Research

Michael Talbot: *The Holographic Universe*

Greg Braden: *Awakening to Zero Point; Walking Between Worlds;
The Isaiah Effect*
Joseph Chilton Pearce: *The Biology of Transcendence*
Phyllis V Schlemmer: *The Only Planet of Choice*
Alice Bailey: *Esoteric Healing, Esoteric Psychology*
Barbara Marciniak: *Earth; Bringers of the Dawn*
Emoto Masaru: *Message from Water*
Jonathan Goldman: *Healing Sounds*
Mark Prophet and Elizabeth: *Saint Germain on Alchemy*
Melissa Gayle: *Exploring the Labyrinth*
Sig Longren: *Labyrinths, Ancient and Modern Uses*

Astrology

There are many excellent astrology writers who have offered me
inspiration through their elegant expertise. To name just a few:

Howard Sasportas
Liz Greene
Erin Sullivan
Noel Tyl
Jan Spiller
Melanie Reinhart
Julia Parker
Darby Costello
Dane Rudhyar

Numerology

Faith Javane and Dusty Bunker: *Numerology and the
Divine Triangle*
Dan Millman: *The Life You Were Born to Live; The Way of the
Peaceful Warrior; The Laws of Spirit*
Juno Jordan: *Your Right Action Number*
Gerie Bauer: *Numerology for Beginners*

Index